50 Whole Meal Recipes for Home

By: Kelly Johnson

Table of Contents

- Roasted Vegetable Quinoa Salad
- Baked Lemon Herb Chicken with Asparagus
- Stuffed Bell Peppers with Brown Rice
- Grilled Salmon with Avocado Salsa
- Lentil and Vegetable Stew
- Chicken and Broccoli Stir-Fry
- Chickpea and Spinach Curry
- Spaghetti Squash with Tomato Basil Sauce
- Turkey and Sweet Potato Skillet
- Shrimp and Zucchini Noodles
- Black Bean and Corn Tacos
- Greek Chicken and Quinoa Bowl
- Mushroom and Barley Risotto
- Tofu and Vegetable Stir-Fry
- Baked Cod with Cherry Tomatoes
- Butternut Squash and Kale Pasta
- Grilled Vegetable and Hummus Wrap
- Chicken and Wild Rice Soup
- Eggplant Parmesan with Whole Wheat Pasta
- Beef and Broccoli Stir-Fry
- Spinach and Feta Stuffed Chicken
- Cauliflower Fried Rice
- Salmon and Sweet Potato Cakes
- Turkey and Vegetable Meatloaf
- Quinoa and Black Bean Stuffed Peppers
- Chicken and Vegetable Kabobs
- Moroccan Chickpea Stew
- Grilled Steak with Chimichurri Sauce
- Vegetable and Lentil Shepherd's Pie
- Shrimp and Avocado Salad
- Chicken and Spinach Alfredo
- Baked Eggplant with Tomato Sauce
- Spicy Tofu and Vegetable Stir-Fry
- Lemon Garlic Shrimp with Zoodles
- Turkey and Kale Chili

- Grilled Portobello Mushroom Burger
- Spinach and Ricotta Stuffed Shells
- Chicken and Sweet Potato Curry
- Zucchini and Corn Fritters
- Baked Tilapia with Steamed Vegetables
- Quinoa and Avocado Salad
- Grilled Lamb Chops with Mint Yogurt
- Roasted Brussels Sprouts and Bacon
- Beef and Vegetable Skillet
- Chicken Caesar Salad Wrap
- Tofu and Vegetable Kebabs
- Barley and Mushroom Soup
- Stuffed Acorn Squash
- Grilled Chicken with Mango Salsa
- Baked Spaghetti with Spinach and Ricotta

Roasted Vegetable Quinoa Salad

Ingredients:

- 1 cup quinoa, rinsed
- 2 cups water or vegetable broth
- 1 red bell pepper, diced
- 1 yellow bell pepper, diced
- 1 zucchini, diced
- 1 red onion, diced
- 1 cup cherry tomatoes, halved
- 2 tablespoons olive oil
- Salt and pepper, to taste
- 1 teaspoon dried oregano
- 1 teaspoon garlic powder
- 1 cup canned chickpeas, rinsed and drained
- 1/4 cup fresh parsley, chopped
- 1/4 cup fresh basil, chopped
- 1/4 cup crumbled feta cheese (optional)
- Juice of 1 lemon

Instructions:

1. Preheat the oven to 425°F (220°C).
2. Cook the quinoa:
    - In a medium saucepan, bring the quinoa and water (or vegetable broth) to a boil.
    - Reduce the heat to low, cover, and simmer for about 15 minutes or until the quinoa is cooked and the water is absorbed.
    - Remove from heat and fluff with a fork. Set aside to cool.
3. Roast the vegetables:
    - On a large baking sheet, toss the diced bell peppers, zucchini, red onion, and cherry tomatoes with olive oil, salt, pepper, oregano, and garlic powder.
    - Spread the vegetables in a single layer and roast in the preheated oven for about 20-25 minutes, or until they are tender and slightly caramelized. Stir halfway through roasting for even cooking.
4. Assemble the salad:
    - In a large bowl, combine the cooked quinoa, roasted vegetables, chickpeas, parsley, and basil.
    - If using, add the crumbled feta cheese.
5. Dress the salad:
    - Squeeze the lemon juice over the salad and toss to combine.
    - Taste and adjust the seasoning with salt and pepper if needed.
6. Serve:
    - The salad can be served warm or chilled. Enjoy as a main dish or a side.

This roasted vegetable quinoa salad is versatile and can be adapted with your favorite vegetables and herbs.

Baked Lemon Herb Chicken with Asparagus

Ingredients:

- 4 boneless, skinless chicken breasts
- 1 bunch asparagus, trimmed
- 2 tablespoons olive oil
- Juice of 2 lemons
- Zest of 1 lemon
- 3 cloves garlic, minced
- 1 teaspoon dried thyme
- 1 teaspoon dried rosemary
- 1 teaspoon dried oregano
- Salt and pepper, to taste
- Lemon slices, for garnish (optional)
- Fresh parsley, chopped (optional)

Instructions:

1. Preheat the oven to 400°F (200°C).
2. Prepare the marinade:
    - In a small bowl, whisk together the olive oil, lemon juice, lemon zest, minced garlic, dried thyme, dried rosemary, dried oregano, salt, and pepper.
3. Marinate the chicken:
    - Place the chicken breasts in a large resealable plastic bag or a shallow dish.
    - Pour the marinade over the chicken, ensuring each piece is well coated.
    - Let it marinate for at least 30 minutes, or up to 2 hours in the refrigerator.
4. Bake the chicken and asparagus:
    - Arrange the marinated chicken breasts on one side of a large baking sheet.
    - Place the asparagus on the other side of the baking sheet.
    - Drizzle a little olive oil over the asparagus and season with salt and pepper.
    - If desired, place lemon slices on top of the chicken breasts for added flavor and presentation.
5. Bake in the preheated oven for 20-25 minutes, or until the chicken is cooked through (internal temperature reaches 165°F or 75°C) and the asparagus is tender.
6. Garnish and serve:
    - Remove from the oven and let the chicken rest for a few minutes.
    - Sprinkle fresh parsley over the chicken and asparagus before serving, if desired.
7. Serve:
    - Plate the chicken breasts and asparagus together, and enjoy with a side of your choice, such as quinoa, brown rice, or a fresh salad.

This baked lemon herb chicken with asparagus is a simple, healthy, and flavorful meal perfect for any night of the week.

Stuffed Bell Peppers with Brown Rice

Ingredients:

- 6 bell peppers (any color), tops cut off and seeds removed
- 1 cup brown rice
- 2 cups vegetable broth or water
- 1 tablespoon olive oil
- 1 onion, finely chopped
- 2 cloves garlic, minced
- 1 zucchini, diced
- 1 can (15 oz) black beans, rinsed and drained
- 1 can (14.5 oz) diced tomatoes, drained
- 1 teaspoon ground cumin
- 1 teaspoon chili powder
- 1 teaspoon dried oregano
- Salt and pepper, to taste
- 1 cup shredded cheddar cheese (optional)
- Fresh cilantro, chopped (optional)

Instructions:

1. Preheat the oven to 375°F (190°C).
2. Cook the brown rice:
    - In a medium saucepan, bring the brown rice and vegetable broth (or water) to a boil.
    - Reduce the heat to low, cover, and simmer for about 45 minutes, or until the rice is cooked and the liquid is absorbed.
    - Remove from heat and set aside.
3. Prepare the filling:
    - In a large skillet, heat the olive oil over medium heat.
    - Add the chopped onion and cook for about 5 minutes, or until softened.
    - Add the minced garlic and cook for another 1-2 minutes, until fragrant.
    - Add the diced zucchini and cook for about 5 minutes, until tender.
    - Stir in the black beans, diced tomatoes, cooked brown rice, ground cumin, chili powder, dried oregano, salt, and pepper.
    - Cook for another 5 minutes, stirring occasionally, until everything is well combined and heated through.
4. Stuff the peppers:
    - Arrange the bell peppers upright in a baking dish.
    - Spoon the filling mixture into each bell pepper, packing it down slightly.
    - If desired, sprinkle shredded cheddar cheese on top of each stuffed pepper.
5. Bake:
    - Cover the baking dish with aluminum foil.
    - Bake in the preheated oven for 30 minutes.

    - Remove the foil and bake for an additional 10-15 minutes, or until the peppers are tender and the cheese is melted and bubbly (if using).
6. Garnish and serve:
    - Remove from the oven and let the peppers cool slightly.
    - Garnish with chopped fresh cilantro, if desired.
7. Serve:
    - Plate the stuffed bell peppers and enjoy!

This stuffed bell peppers recipe is versatile and can be adjusted to include your favorite vegetables and spices. It makes for a hearty and nutritious meal.

Grilled Salmon with Avocado Salsa

Ingredients:

For the Salmon:

- 4 salmon fillets (about 6 ounces each)
- 2 tablespoons olive oil
- Juice of 1 lime
- 1 teaspoon ground cumin
- 1 teaspoon smoked paprika
- 1/2 teaspoon garlic powder
- Salt and pepper, to taste

For the Avocado Salsa:

- 2 ripe avocados, diced
- 1 small red onion, finely chopped
- 1 jalapeño, seeded and finely chopped
- 1/4 cup fresh cilantro, chopped
- Juice of 1 lime
- Salt and pepper, to taste

Instructions:

1. Prepare the salmon:
   - In a small bowl, combine the olive oil, lime juice, ground cumin, smoked paprika, garlic powder, salt, and pepper.
   - Rub this mixture all over the salmon fillets, making sure they are evenly coated.
   - Let the salmon marinate for about 15-20 minutes.
2. Make the avocado salsa:
   - In a medium bowl, gently combine the diced avocados, chopped red onion, chopped jalapeño, chopped cilantro, lime juice, salt, and pepper.
   - Mix carefully to avoid mashing the avocados.
   - Adjust seasoning to taste and set aside.
3. Grill the salmon:
   - Preheat the grill to medium-high heat.
   - Lightly oil the grill grates to prevent sticking.
   - Place the salmon fillets on the grill, skin side down if the skin is on.
   - Grill for about 4-5 minutes per side, depending on the thickness of the fillets, until the salmon is cooked through and flakes easily with a fork.
4. Serve:
   - Transfer the grilled salmon to a serving platter.
   - Spoon the avocado salsa over the top of each salmon fillet.
5. Garnish:

- Optionally, garnish with additional lime wedges and fresh cilantro.
6. Enjoy:
    - Serve immediately with your favorite sides, such as a fresh green salad, grilled vegetables, or rice.

This Grilled Salmon with Avocado Salsa is a refreshing and healthy meal that's perfect for any occasion!

Lentil and Vegetable Stew

Ingredients:

- 1 tablespoon olive oil
- 1 large onion, chopped
- 3 cloves garlic, minced
- 2 carrots, diced
- 2 celery stalks, diced
- 1 bell pepper, diced
- 1 zucchini, diced
- 1 cup dried brown or green lentils, rinsed
- 1 can (14.5 oz) diced tomatoes, with juice
- 6 cups vegetable broth
- 1 teaspoon ground cumin
- 1 teaspoon dried thyme
- 1 teaspoon smoked paprika
- 1 bay leaf
- Salt and pepper, to taste
- 2 cups chopped kale or spinach
- 2 tablespoons fresh parsley, chopped (optional)
- Juice of 1 lemon

Instructions:

1. Prepare the vegetables:
    - Chop the onion, garlic, carrots, celery, bell pepper, and zucchini. Set aside.
2. Cook the aromatics:
    - In a large pot, heat the olive oil over medium heat.
    - Add the chopped onion and cook for about 5 minutes, until softened.
    - Add the minced garlic and cook for another 1-2 minutes, until fragrant.
3. Add the vegetables:
    - Stir in the carrots, celery, bell pepper, and zucchini.
    - Cook for about 5-7 minutes, until the vegetables begin to soften.
4. Add the lentils and tomatoes:
    - Stir in the lentils and the can of diced tomatoes with their juice.
5. Add the broth and seasonings:
    - Pour in the vegetable broth.
    - Add the ground cumin, dried thyme, smoked paprika, bay leaf, salt, and pepper.
    - Stir well to combine.
6. Simmer the stew:
    - Bring the mixture to a boil.
    - Reduce the heat to low, cover, and simmer for about 30-35 minutes, or until the lentils are tender and the flavors have melded together.
7. Add the greens:

- Stir in the chopped kale or spinach.
- Simmer for another 5-10 minutes, until the greens are wilted and tender.
8. Finish the stew:
    - Remove the bay leaf.
    - Stir in the fresh parsley (if using) and the lemon juice.
    - Adjust seasoning with additional salt and pepper, if needed.
9. Serve:
    - Ladle the lentil and vegetable stew into bowls.
    - Serve hot, optionally with a side of crusty bread or over cooked rice.

This Lentil and Vegetable Stew is perfect for a comforting and healthy meal, packed with nutrients and flavors!

Chicken and Broccoli Stir-Fry

Ingredients:

- 2 tablespoons vegetable oil
- 1 pound boneless, skinless chicken breasts, thinly sliced
- 2 cups broccoli florets
- 1 red bell pepper, thinly sliced
- 1 onion, thinly sliced
- 3 cloves garlic, minced
- 1 tablespoon fresh ginger, grated
- 1/4 cup soy sauce (or tamari for gluten-free)
- 2 tablespoons oyster sauce (optional)
- 2 tablespoons hoisin sauce
- 1 tablespoon cornstarch mixed with 2 tablespoons water
- 1/4 cup chicken broth or water
- 2 tablespoons sesame oil
- 1 teaspoon sesame seeds (optional)
- 2 green onions, chopped (optional)
- Cooked rice or noodles, for serving

Instructions:

1. Prepare the sauce:
    - In a small bowl, mix together the soy sauce, oyster sauce (if using), hoisin sauce, and chicken broth (or water).
    - Set aside.
2. Cook the chicken:
    - Heat 1 tablespoon of vegetable oil in a large skillet or wok over medium-high heat.
    - Add the thinly sliced chicken and cook until browned and cooked through, about 5-7 minutes.
    - Remove the chicken from the skillet and set aside.
3. Stir-fry the vegetables:
    - In the same skillet, add the remaining 1 tablespoon of vegetable oil.
    - Add the broccoli florets, red bell pepper, and onion. Stir-fry for about 5 minutes, until the vegetables are tender-crisp.
    - Add the minced garlic and grated ginger, and stir-fry for another 1-2 minutes, until fragrant.
4. Combine chicken and sauce:
    - Return the cooked chicken to the skillet with the vegetables.
    - Pour the prepared sauce over the chicken and vegetables.
    - Stir to coat everything evenly.
5. Thicken the sauce:

- Add the cornstarch mixture (1 tablespoon cornstarch mixed with 2 tablespoons water) to the skillet.
- Stir well and cook for another 2-3 minutes, until the sauce has thickened.
6. Finish the stir-fry:
    - Drizzle the sesame oil over the stir-fry.
    - Stir in the sesame seeds and chopped green onions, if using.
7. Serve:
    - Serve the chicken and broccoli stir-fry hot over cooked rice or noodles.

This Chicken and Broccoli Stir-Fry is a quick, healthy, and flavorful meal perfect for busy weeknights!

Chickpea and Spinach Curry

Ingredients:

- 2 tablespoons vegetable oil
- 1 large onion, finely chopped
- 3 cloves garlic, minced
- 1 tablespoon fresh ginger, grated
- 1-2 green chilies, finely chopped (optional)
- 1 tablespoon ground cumin
- 1 tablespoon ground coriander
- 1 teaspoon turmeric powder
- 1 teaspoon garam masala
- 1 teaspoon paprika
- 1 can (14.5 oz) diced tomatoes
- 1 can (15 oz) coconut milk
- 2 cans (15 oz each) chickpeas, rinsed and drained
- 4 cups fresh spinach, roughly chopped
- Salt and pepper, to taste
- Juice of 1 lime
- Fresh cilantro, chopped, for garnish

Instructions:

1. Cook the aromatics:
    - Heat the vegetable oil in a large pot or skillet over medium heat.
    - Add the finely chopped onion and cook for about 5 minutes, until softened and translucent.
    - Add the minced garlic, grated ginger, and chopped green chilies (if using). Cook for another 1-2 minutes, until fragrant.
2. Add the spices:
    - Stir in the ground cumin, ground coriander, turmeric powder, garam masala, and paprika.
    - Cook for about 1 minute, stirring constantly, to toast the spices and release their flavors.
3. Add the tomatoes and coconut milk:
    - Pour in the diced tomatoes and coconut milk.
    - Stir well to combine, bringing the mixture to a gentle simmer.
4. Add the chickpeas:
    - Stir in the rinsed and drained chickpeas.
    - Let the curry simmer for about 10-15 minutes, allowing the flavors to meld together and the chickpeas to heat through.
5. Add the spinach:
    - Add the roughly chopped spinach to the pot.
    - Stir well, allowing the spinach to wilt and incorporate into the curry.

6. Season and finish:
    - Season the curry with salt and pepper to taste.
    - Stir in the juice of 1 lime to add brightness and balance the flavors.
7. Garnish and serve:
    - Remove from heat and garnish with chopped fresh cilantro.
    - Serve the chickpea and spinach curry hot, with rice, naan, or your favorite flatbread.

This Chickpea and Spinach Curry is a flavorful and wholesome dish that's perfect for a hearty meal any day of the week!

Spaghetti Squash with Tomato Basil Sauce

Ingredients:

For the Spaghetti Squash:

- 1 large spaghetti squash
- 2 tablespoons olive oil
- Salt and pepper, to taste

For the Tomato Basil Sauce:

- 2 tablespoons olive oil
- 1 large onion, finely chopped
- 4 cloves garlic, minced
- 1 can (28 oz) crushed tomatoes
- 1 can (14.5 oz) diced tomatoes
- 1 teaspoon dried oregano
- 1 teaspoon dried basil
- 1/2 teaspoon red pepper flakes (optional)
- Salt and pepper, to taste
- 1/4 cup fresh basil leaves, chopped
- 1 teaspoon sugar (optional)

Instructions:

1. Prepare the spaghetti squash:
    - Preheat your oven to 400°F (200°C).
    - Carefully cut the spaghetti squash in half lengthwise and scoop out the seeds.
    - Drizzle the insides of the squash halves with olive oil and season with salt and pepper.
    - Place the squash halves cut side down on a baking sheet lined with parchment paper.
    - Roast in the preheated oven for about 40-45 minutes, or until the squash is tender and easily shredded with a fork.
    - Once cooked, let the squash cool slightly. Use a fork to scrape out the flesh into spaghetti-like strands. Set aside.
2. Prepare the tomato basil sauce:
    - In a large skillet or saucepan, heat the olive oil over medium heat.
    - Add the finely chopped onion and cook for about 5 minutes, until softened and translucent.
    - Add the minced garlic and cook for another 1-2 minutes, until fragrant.
    - Stir in the crushed tomatoes and diced tomatoes, and bring the mixture to a simmer.
    - Add the dried oregano, dried basil, red pepper flakes (if using), salt, and pepper.

- Simmer the sauce for about 20-25 minutes, stirring occasionally, until it thickens and the flavors meld together.
            - Taste and adjust seasoning as needed. If the sauce is too acidic, you can add a teaspoon of sugar to balance it out.
            - Stir in the fresh chopped basil leaves just before serving.
    3. Combine and serve:
        - Divide the spaghetti squash strands among serving plates.
        - Spoon the tomato basil sauce over the spaghetti squash.
        - Garnish with additional fresh basil, if desired.
    4. Enjoy:
        - Serve hot, optionally with a side of garlic bread or a fresh green salad.

This Spaghetti Squash with Tomato Basil Sauce is a light, flavorful, and nutritious alternative to traditional pasta dishes!

Turkey and Sweet Potato Skillet

Ingredients:

- 1 tablespoon olive oil
- 1 pound ground turkey
- 2 medium sweet potatoes, peeled and diced
- 1 onion, diced
- 2 cloves garlic, minced
- 1 red bell pepper, diced
- 1 teaspoon ground cumin
- 1 teaspoon paprika
- 1/2 teaspoon chili powder (adjust to taste)
- Salt and pepper, to taste
- 1 cup chicken broth
- 2 cups fresh spinach leaves
- 1/4 cup chopped fresh cilantro (optional)
- Juice of 1 lime

Instructions:

1. Brown the turkey:
   - Heat the olive oil in a large skillet over medium-high heat.
   - Add the ground turkey to the skillet, breaking it apart with a spoon, and cook until browned and cooked through. Remove from skillet and set aside.
2. Cook the sweet potatoes and onions:
   - In the same skillet, add the diced sweet potatoes and diced onion.
   - Cook for about 5-7 minutes, stirring occasionally, until the sweet potatoes are slightly tender and the onions are translucent.
3. Add the aromatics and spices:
   - Add the minced garlic and diced red bell pepper to the skillet.
   - Cook for another 2-3 minutes until the peppers are softened and the garlic is fragrant.
   - Stir in the ground cumin, paprika, chili powder, salt, and pepper. Cook for another minute until the spices are fragrant.
4. Combine and simmer:
   - Return the cooked ground turkey to the skillet and stir to combine with the vegetables.
   - Pour in the chicken broth and bring the mixture to a simmer.
   - Reduce the heat to medium-low and let the mixture simmer for about 10-15 minutes, or until the sweet potatoes are tender and the flavors have melded together.
5. Add spinach and finish:
   - Stir in the fresh spinach leaves and let them wilt in the skillet.
   - Once the spinach is wilted, remove the skillet from heat.

- Squeeze the juice of one lime over the skillet and stir to combine.
        - If desired, garnish with chopped fresh cilantro before serving.
6. Serve:
    - Serve the turkey and sweet potato skillet hot, optionally with a side of rice or quinoa.

This Turkey and Sweet Potato Skillet is a flavorful and nutritious one-pan meal that's perfect for a quick and satisfying dinner!

Shrimp and Zucchini Noodles

Ingredients:

- 1 pound large shrimp, peeled and deveined
- 3 medium zucchinis
- 2 tablespoons olive oil
- 4 cloves garlic, minced
- 1 teaspoon red pepper flakes (adjust to taste)
- Salt and pepper, to taste
- Juice of 1 lemon
- 2 tablespoons chopped fresh parsley
- Grated Parmesan cheese, for serving (optional)

Instructions:

1. Prepare the zucchini noodles:
    - Using a spiralizer or a vegetable peeler, spiralize or julienne the zucchinis into noodles.
    - Set aside.
2. Cook the shrimp:
    - Heat 1 tablespoon of olive oil in a large skillet over medium-high heat.
    - Add the peeled and deveined shrimp to the skillet.
    - Cook the shrimp for 2-3 minutes on each side, or until they are pink and opaque.
    - Once cooked, remove the shrimp from the skillet and set aside.
3. Make the sauce:
    - In the same skillet, heat the remaining 1 tablespoon of olive oil over medium heat.
    - Add the minced garlic and red pepper flakes to the skillet.
    - Cook for 1-2 minutes, stirring constantly, until the garlic is fragrant but not browned.
4. Cook the zucchini noodles:
    - Add the zucchini noodles to the skillet.
    - Season with salt and pepper to taste.
    - Cook the zucchini noodles for 2-3 minutes, tossing occasionally, until they are just tender but still crisp.
5. Combine and finish:
    - Return the cooked shrimp to the skillet with the zucchini noodles.
    - Drizzle the lemon juice over the shrimp and zucchini noodles.
    - Add the chopped fresh parsley and toss everything together to combine.
    - Taste and adjust seasoning if necessary.
6. Serve:
    - Serve the shrimp and zucchini noodles hot, optionally garnished with grated Parmesan cheese.

This Shrimp and Zucchini Noodles recipe is a light, healthy, and flavorful dish that's perfect for a quick and satisfying meal!

Black Bean and Corn Tacos

Ingredients:

For the Filling:

- 1 tablespoon olive oil
- 1 small onion, finely chopped
- 3 cloves garlic, minced
- 1 red bell pepper, diced
- 1 can (15 oz) black beans, rinsed and drained
- 1 cup corn kernels (fresh, frozen, or canned)
- 1 teaspoon ground cumin
- 1 teaspoon chili powder
- 1/2 teaspoon smoked paprika
- Salt and pepper, to taste
- Juice of 1 lime
- 1/4 cup fresh cilantro, chopped

For Serving:

- 8 small corn or flour tortillas
- 1 cup shredded lettuce
- 1/2 cup diced tomatoes
- 1/2 cup diced red onion
- 1/2 cup crumbled feta or cotija cheese
- 1 avocado, sliced
- Salsa or hot sauce (optional)
- Lime wedges

Instructions:

1. Prepare the filling:
    - Heat the olive oil in a large skillet over medium heat.
    - Add the finely chopped onion and cook for about 5 minutes, until softened.
    - Add the minced garlic and diced red bell pepper, and cook for another 2-3 minutes, until the bell pepper is tender.
    - Stir in the black beans, corn kernels, ground cumin, chili powder, smoked paprika, salt, and pepper.
    - Cook for about 5-7 minutes, stirring occasionally, until the mixture is heated through and well combined.
    - Remove from heat and stir in the lime juice and chopped fresh cilantro.
2. Warm the tortillas:
    - Heat the tortillas in a dry skillet over medium heat for about 30 seconds on each side, or until warm and pliable.

- Alternatively, wrap the tortillas in aluminum foil and warm them in a preheated oven at 350°F (175°C) for about 10 minutes.
3. Assemble the tacos:
    - Divide the black bean and corn filling evenly among the warmed tortillas.
    - Top each taco with shredded lettuce, diced tomatoes, diced red onion, crumbled feta or cotija cheese, and avocado slices.
    - Add salsa or hot sauce if desired.
4. Serve:
    - Serve the tacos with lime wedges on the side for an extra burst of flavor.

These Black Bean and Corn Tacos are a flavorful and nutritious meal that's easy to prepare and perfect for a quick lunch or dinner!

Greek Chicken and Quinoa Bowl

Ingredients:

For the Chicken Marinade:

- 1 pound boneless, skinless chicken breasts
- 3 tablespoons olive oil
- Juice of 1 lemon
- 2 cloves garlic, minced
- 1 teaspoon dried oregano
- 1/2 teaspoon dried thyme
- Salt and pepper, to taste

For the Quinoa:

- 1 cup quinoa
- 2 cups water or chicken broth
- Pinch of salt

For the Toppings:

- 1 cucumber, diced
- 1 cup cherry tomatoes, halved
- 1/4 red onion, thinly sliced
- 1/2 cup kalamata olives, pitted and sliced
- 1/2 cup crumbled feta cheese
- 1/4 cup fresh parsley, chopped

For the Dressing:

- 3 tablespoons olive oil
- 2 tablespoons red wine vinegar
- 1 tablespoon lemon juice
- 1 teaspoon dried oregano
- Salt and pepper, to taste

Instructions:

1. Marinate the chicken:
   - In a bowl, combine the olive oil, lemon juice, minced garlic, dried oregano, dried thyme, salt, and pepper.
   - Add the chicken breasts, ensuring they are well coated with the marinade.
   - Cover and refrigerate for at least 30 minutes, or up to 2 hours.
2. Cook the quinoa:
   - Rinse the quinoa under cold water.

- In a medium saucepan, bring 2 cups of water or chicken broth to a boil.
- Add a pinch of salt and the rinsed quinoa.
- Reduce the heat to low, cover, and simmer for about 15 minutes, or until the quinoa is cooked and the liquid is absorbed.
- Remove from heat and let it sit, covered, for 5 minutes.
- Fluff with a fork and set aside.

3. Cook the chicken:
   - Preheat a grill or a skillet over medium-high heat.
   - Cook the marinated chicken breasts for about 6-7 minutes per side, or until fully cooked and the internal temperature reaches 165°F (75°C).
   - Remove from heat and let the chicken rest for a few minutes before slicing.
4. Prepare the dressing:
   - In a small bowl, whisk together the olive oil, red wine vinegar, lemon juice, dried oregano, salt, and pepper.
   - Set aside.
5. Assemble the bowls:
   - Divide the cooked quinoa among four bowls.
   - Top each bowl with sliced chicken, diced cucumber, cherry tomato halves, thinly sliced red onion, kalamata olives, crumbled feta cheese, and chopped fresh parsley.
6. Drizzle with dressing:
   - Drizzle the prepared dressing over each bowl.
   - Toss gently to combine, if desired.
7. Serve:
   - Serve immediately, with extra dressing on the side if needed.

This Greek Chicken and Quinoa Bowl is a healthy, balanced meal packed with flavors and nutrients, perfect for a satisfying lunch or dinner!

Mushroom and Barley Risotto

Ingredients:

- 2 tablespoons olive oil
- 1 small onion, finely chopped
- 2 cloves garlic, minced
- 1 cup pearl barley
- 8 ounces mushrooms (such as cremini, shiitake, or button), sliced
- 1/2 cup white wine (optional)
- 4 cups vegetable broth, warmed
- 1/2 cup grated Parmesan cheese
- 2 tablespoons butter
- Salt and pepper, to taste
- 2 tablespoons chopped fresh parsley
- 1 teaspoon chopped fresh thyme (or 1/2 teaspoon dried thyme)

Instructions:

1. Prepare the broth:
    - In a saucepan, warm the vegetable broth over low heat. Keep it warm throughout the cooking process.
2. Cook the aromatics:
    - In a large skillet or saucepan, heat the olive oil over medium heat.
    - Add the finely chopped onion and cook for about 5 minutes, until softened and translucent.
    - Add the minced garlic and cook for another 1-2 minutes, until fragrant.
3. Toast the barley:
    - Stir in the pearl barley and cook for about 2-3 minutes, stirring frequently, until the barley is lightly toasted.
4. Cook the mushrooms:
    - Add the sliced mushrooms to the skillet and cook for about 5-7 minutes, until they release their moisture and start to brown.
5. Deglaze with wine (optional):
    - Pour in the white wine and cook for about 2-3 minutes, stirring occasionally, until the wine is mostly absorbed.
6. Add the broth:
    - Begin adding the warm vegetable broth to the barley mixture, one ladleful at a time, stirring frequently.
    - Allow the liquid to be mostly absorbed before adding the next ladleful of broth.
    - Continue this process until the barley is tender and creamy, about 30-40 minutes.
7. Finish the risotto:
    - Once the barley is cooked and the mixture is creamy, stir in the grated Parmesan cheese and butter.
    - Season with salt and pepper to taste.

        - Stir in the chopped fresh parsley and thyme.
  8. Serve:
        - Serve the mushroom and barley risotto hot, garnished with additional fresh herbs and a sprinkle of Parmesan cheese, if desired.

This Mushroom and Barley Risotto is a hearty and flavorful dish that makes a perfect comforting meal!

Tofu and Vegetable Stir-Fry

Ingredients:

For the Stir-Fry:

- 1 block (14 oz) firm tofu, drained and pressed
- 2 tablespoons vegetable oil, divided
- 1 red bell pepper, thinly sliced
- 1 yellow bell pepper, thinly sliced
- 1 medium carrot, julienned
- 1 zucchini, julienned
- 1 cup broccoli florets
- 3 cloves garlic, minced
- 1 tablespoon fresh ginger, minced
- 2 green onions, chopped

For the Sauce:

- 1/4 cup soy sauce (or tamari for gluten-free)
- 2 tablespoons hoisin sauce
- 1 tablespoon rice vinegar
- 1 tablespoon sesame oil
- 1 tablespoon cornstarch mixed with 2 tablespoons water
- 1 teaspoon sriracha or other hot sauce (optional)
- 1 tablespoon honey or maple syrup (optional)

For Serving:

- Cooked rice or noodles
- Sesame seeds (optional)
- Additional chopped green onions (optional)

Instructions:

1. Prepare the tofu:
    - Cut the pressed tofu into 1-inch cubes.
    - Heat 1 tablespoon of vegetable oil in a large skillet or wok over medium-high heat.
    - Add the tofu cubes and cook until golden brown on all sides, about 5-7 minutes.
    - Remove the tofu from the skillet and set aside.
2. Prepare the sauce:
    - In a small bowl, whisk together the soy sauce, hoisin sauce, rice vinegar, sesame oil, cornstarch mixture, and sriracha (if using).
    - Add honey or maple syrup if you prefer a touch of sweetness. Set aside.
3. Cook the vegetables:

- In the same skillet, add the remaining 1 tablespoon of vegetable oil.
- Add the minced garlic and ginger, and cook for about 1 minute, until fragrant.
- Add the sliced bell peppers, julienned carrot, julienned zucchini, and broccoli florets.
- Stir-fry the vegetables for about 5-7 minutes, until they are tender-crisp.
4. Combine tofu and sauce:
    - Return the cooked tofu to the skillet with the vegetables.
    - Pour the sauce over the tofu and vegetables.
    - Stir well to coat everything evenly.
    - Cook for another 2-3 minutes, until the sauce has thickened and everything is heated through.
5. Serve:
    - Serve the tofu and vegetable stir-fry hot over cooked rice or noodles.
    - Garnish with sesame seeds and additional chopped green onions, if desired.

This Tofu and Vegetable Stir-Fry is a quick, nutritious, and delicious meal that's perfect for a healthy weeknight dinner!

Baked Cod with Cherry Tomatoes

Ingredients:

- 4 cod fillets (about 6 ounces each)
- 2 tablespoons olive oil
- 1 pint cherry tomatoes, halved
- 3 cloves garlic, minced
- 1 lemon, thinly sliced
- 1/4 cup white wine (optional)
- 1/4 cup fresh basil leaves, chopped
- Salt and pepper, to taste
- 1/4 teaspoon red pepper flakes (optional)
- Fresh parsley, chopped, for garnish

Instructions:

1. Preheat the oven:
    - Preheat your oven to 400°F (200°C).
2. Prepare the baking dish:
    - Drizzle 1 tablespoon of olive oil in a large baking dish.
    - Arrange the cod fillets in the baking dish and season them with salt and pepper.
3. Prepare the tomatoes:
    - In a medium bowl, combine the halved cherry tomatoes, minced garlic, remaining 1 tablespoon of olive oil, and red pepper flakes (if using).
    - Toss to coat the tomatoes evenly.
4. Assemble the dish:
    - Spread the tomato mixture around the cod fillets in the baking dish.
    - Place lemon slices over and around the cod fillets.
    - Pour the white wine (if using) around the edges of the baking dish.
5. Bake the cod:
    - Bake in the preheated oven for 15-20 minutes, or until the cod is opaque and flakes easily with a fork.
    - Cooking time may vary slightly depending on the thickness of the fillets.
6. Add the basil:
    - Once the cod is cooked, remove the baking dish from the oven.
    - Sprinkle the chopped fresh basil over the baked cod and tomatoes.
7. Serve:
    - Transfer the cod fillets to serving plates.
    - Spoon the cherry tomatoes and pan juices over the cod.
    - Garnish with chopped fresh parsley.
8. Optional sides:
    - Serve with a side of steamed vegetables, a fresh green salad, or crusty bread to soak up the delicious juices.

This Baked Cod with Cherry Tomatoes is a light, flavorful, and healthy dish that's perfect for a quick and easy weeknight dinner!

Butternut Squash and Kale Pasta

Ingredients

- 1 medium butternut squash, peeled and diced
- 2 tablespoons olive oil
- Salt and pepper, to taste
- 12 ounces pasta (such as penne or fusilli)
- 1 bunch kale, stems removed and leaves chopped
- 4 cloves garlic, minced
- 1/2 teaspoon red pepper flakes (optional)
- 1/2 cup grated Parmesan cheese (or a vegan alternative)
- 1/4 cup pine nuts, toasted (optional)
- Zest and juice of 1 lemon

Instructions

1. Roast the Butternut Squash:
   - Preheat your oven to 400°F (200°C).
   - Toss the diced butternut squash with 1 tablespoon of olive oil, salt, and pepper.
   - Spread it out on a baking sheet and roast for 25-30 minutes, or until tender and slightly caramelized. Stir halfway through for even cooking.
2. Cook the Pasta:
   - While the squash is roasting, cook the pasta in a large pot of salted boiling water according to the package instructions. Reserve 1 cup of pasta water, then drain the pasta.
3. Prepare the Kale:
   - In a large skillet, heat the remaining tablespoon of olive oil over medium heat.
   - Add the minced garlic and red pepper flakes, cooking until fragrant (about 1 minute).
   - Add the chopped kale and a pinch of salt. Cook, stirring frequently, until the kale is wilted and tender, about 5-7 minutes.
4. Combine Ingredients:
   - Add the roasted butternut squash to the skillet with the kale.
   - Add the cooked pasta to the skillet, along with a splash of the reserved pasta water to help everything come together.
   - Stir in the Parmesan cheese, lemon zest, and lemon juice. Mix well to combine. Add more pasta water if the mixture seems dry.
5. Serve:
   - Serve the pasta hot, topped with toasted pine nuts if using, and extra grated Parmesan cheese on the side.

Enjoy your Butternut Squash and Kale Pasta!

Grilled Vegetable and Hummus Wrap

Ingredients

- 1 red bell pepper, sliced into strips
- 1 zucchini, sliced lengthwise
- 1 yellow squash, sliced lengthwise
- 1 red onion, sliced into rings
- 1 eggplant, sliced into rounds
- 2 tablespoons olive oil
- Salt and pepper, to taste
- 1 teaspoon dried oregano (optional)
- 4 large whole wheat tortillas or wraps
- 1 cup hummus (store-bought or homemade)
- 1 cup baby spinach or mixed greens
- 1/2 cup crumbled feta cheese (optional)
- 1/4 cup chopped fresh basil or parsley (optional)
- Balsamic glaze or vinegar, for drizzling (optional)

Instructions

1. Prepare the Vegetables:
    - Preheat your grill or grill pan over medium-high heat.
    - Toss the sliced bell pepper, zucchini, yellow squash, red onion, and eggplant with olive oil, salt, pepper, and dried oregano if using.
2. Grill the Vegetables:
    - Grill the vegetables until they are tender and have nice grill marks, about 4-5 minutes per side.
    - Remove from the grill and set aside.
3. Assemble the Wraps:
    - Lay out the tortillas on a clean surface.
    - Spread a generous layer of hummus on each tortilla.
    - Layer the grilled vegetables evenly over the hummus.
    - Add a handful of baby spinach or mixed greens on top of the vegetables.
    - Sprinkle with crumbled feta cheese and chopped fresh herbs, if using.
4. Finish and Serve:
    - Drizzle with balsamic glaze or vinegar, if desired.
    - Roll up the tortillas tightly, folding in the sides as you go to create a wrap.
    - Cut each wrap in half and serve immediately.

Enjoy your Grilled Vegetable and Hummus Wrap!

Chicken and Wild Rice Soup

Ingredients:

- 1 tablespoon olive oil
- 1 onion, finely chopped
- 2 carrots, diced
- 2 celery stalks, diced
- 2 cloves garlic, minced
- 1 teaspoon dried thyme
- 1 teaspoon dried rosemary
- Salt and pepper to taste
- 1 cup wild rice
- 6 cups chicken broth
- 2 boneless, skinless chicken breasts, cooked and shredded
- 1 cup heavy cream or half-and-half
- Fresh parsley, chopped, for garnish

Instructions:

1. Sauté Vegetables:
    - Heat olive oil in a large pot over medium heat. Add onions, carrots, and celery. Sauté until vegetables are tender, about 5-7 minutes.
    - Add minced garlic, thyme, rosemary, salt, and pepper. Cook for another 2 minutes until fragrant.
2. Add Rice and Broth:
    - Stir in wild rice and chicken broth. Bring to a boil, then reduce heat to low and simmer, covered, for 45-50 minutes, or until rice is tender.
3. Add Chicken:
    - Add shredded chicken to the pot and simmer for an additional 10 minutes to heat through.
4. Add Cream:
    - Stir in heavy cream or half-and-half. Simmer for another 5 minutes, stirring occasionally.
5. Adjust Seasoning and Serve:
    - Taste and adjust seasoning with more salt and pepper if necessary.
    - Serve hot, garnished with chopped fresh parsley.

Enjoy your delicious and hearty chicken and wild rice soup!

Eggplant Parmesan with Whole Wheat Pasta

Ingredients:

For Eggplant Parmesan:

- 2 medium eggplants, sliced into 1/2-inch rounds
- 2 cups whole wheat breadcrumbs
- 1 cup grated Parmesan cheese
- 2 eggs, beaten
- 2 cups marinara sauce
- 2 cups shredded mozzarella cheese
- Salt and pepper, to taste
- Olive oil, for frying

For Whole Wheat Pasta:

- 12 ounces whole wheat pasta (such as spaghetti or penne)
- Salt, for boiling water

Instructions:

For Eggplant Parmesan:

1. Preheat Oven: Preheat the oven to 375°F (190°C).
2. Prepare Eggplant: Season the eggplant slices with salt and pepper. Set up a breading station with beaten eggs in one bowl and a mixture of breadcrumbs and grated Parmesan cheese in another.
3. Bread Eggplant: Dip each eggplant slice in the beaten eggs, then coat with the breadcrumb and Parmesan mixture, pressing gently to adhere.
4. Fry Eggplant: Heat olive oil in a large skillet over medium-high heat. Fry the breaded eggplant slices in batches until golden brown on both sides, about 2-3 minutes per side. Transfer to a paper towel-lined plate to drain excess oil.
5. Assemble Eggplant Parmesan: Spread a thin layer of marinara sauce in the bottom of a baking dish. Arrange a layer of fried eggplant slices on top of the sauce. Spoon more marinara sauce over the eggplant, then sprinkle with shredded mozzarella cheese. Repeat the layers until all ingredients are used, finishing with a layer of mozzarella cheese on top.
6. Bake: Cover the baking dish with aluminum foil and bake in the preheated oven for 25-30 minutes, or until the cheese is melted and bubbly.

For Whole Wheat Pasta:

1. Cook Pasta: Bring a large pot of salted water to a boil. Add the whole wheat pasta and cook according to package instructions until al dente. Drain the pasta.

2. Serve: Serve the Eggplant Parmesan hot with the whole wheat pasta on the side. Garnish with fresh basil or parsley, if desired.

Enjoy your Eggplant Parmesan with Whole Wheat Pasta!

Beef and Broccoli Stir-Fry

Ingredients:

For the Stir-Fry Sauce:

- 1/4 cup soy sauce (or tamari for gluten-free option)
- 2 tablespoons oyster sauce
- 1 tablespoon hoisin sauce
- 1 tablespoon rice vinegar
- 2 teaspoons sesame oil
- 2 teaspoons cornstarch
- 1/4 cup water

For the Stir-Fry:

- 1 lb (450g) flank steak or sirloin, thinly sliced against the grain
- 2 tablespoons vegetable oil, divided
- 3 cloves garlic, minced
- 1 teaspoon fresh ginger, grated
- 1 head broccoli, cut into florets
- 1 medium onion, sliced
- Cooked rice or noodles, for serving

Instructions:

1. Prepare the Stir-Fry Sauce:
   - In a small bowl, whisk together soy sauce, oyster sauce, hoisin sauce, rice vinegar, sesame oil, cornstarch, and water until well combined. Set aside.
2. Marinate the Beef:
   - Place the thinly sliced beef in a bowl and pour half of the prepared stir-fry sauce over it. Toss to coat the beef evenly. Let it marinate for at least 15-30 minutes.
3. Cook the Broccoli:
   - Heat 1 tablespoon of vegetable oil in a large skillet or wok over medium-high heat. Add minced garlic and grated ginger, and cook for about 30 seconds until fragrant.
   - Add the broccoli florets and sliced onion to the skillet. Stir-fry for 3-4 minutes until the broccoli is crisp-tender. Remove the cooked broccoli and onion from the skillet and set aside.
4. Cook the Beef:
   - In the same skillet, heat the remaining tablespoon of vegetable oil over high heat. Add the marinated beef slices in a single layer. Cook for 2-3 minutes without stirring to allow the beef to sear and brown.
   - Stir-fry the beef for another 2-3 minutes until cooked through.
5. Combine and Serve:

- Return the cooked broccoli and onion to the skillet with the beef.
- Pour the remaining stir-fry sauce over the beef and vegetables. Stir well to coat everything evenly and allow the sauce to thicken.
- Cook for another minute until heated through.
- Serve the beef and broccoli stir-fry hot over cooked rice or noodles.

Enjoy your flavorful Beef and Broccoli Stir-Fry!

Spinach and Feta Stuffed Chicken

Ingredients:

- 4 boneless, skinless chicken breasts
- 1 cup frozen spinach, thawed and drained
- 1/2 cup crumbled feta cheese
- 2 cloves garlic, minced
- 1 tablespoon olive oil
- Salt and pepper, to taste
- Toothpicks or kitchen twine

Instructions:

1. Preheat Oven: Preheat your oven to 375°F (190°C).
2. Prepare Chicken:
    - Lay the chicken breasts flat on a cutting board. Using a sharp knife, slice a pocket horizontally into the side of each chicken breast, being careful not to cut all the way through. You want to create a pocket for the stuffing.
3. Make the Filling:
    - In a mixing bowl, combine the thawed and drained spinach, crumbled feta cheese, minced garlic, olive oil, salt, and pepper. Mix well to combine.
4. Stuff the Chicken:
    - Divide the spinach and feta mixture evenly among the chicken breasts, spooning it into the pockets you created. Press the openings closed or secure with toothpicks.
5. Season the Chicken:
    - Season the outside of each stuffed chicken breast with a little more salt and pepper, if desired.
6. Cook the Chicken:
    - Heat a large oven-safe skillet over medium-high heat. Once hot, add a little olive oil to the skillet.
    - Carefully place the stuffed chicken breasts in the skillet. Cook for 2-3 minutes on each side until golden brown.
    - Transfer the skillet to the preheated oven and bake for 20-25 minutes, or until the chicken is cooked through and reaches an internal temperature of 165°F (75°C).
7. Rest and Serve:
    - Once cooked, remove the skillet from the oven and let the chicken rest for a few minutes.
    - Remove any toothpicks or twine used for securing the chicken.
    - Serve the spinach and feta stuffed chicken hot, garnished with fresh herbs if desired.

Enjoy your tasty Spinach and Feta Stuffed Chicken!

Cauliflower Fried Rice

Ingredients:

- 1 medium head of cauliflower
- 2 tablespoons sesame oil or vegetable oil
- 2 cloves garlic, minced
- 1 small onion, diced
- 1 cup mixed vegetables (such as carrots, peas, and corn)
- 2 eggs, beaten
- 3 tablespoons soy sauce (or tamari for gluten-free option)
- 1 teaspoon sriracha or chili garlic sauce (optional)
- Salt and pepper, to taste
- Green onions, chopped, for garnish

Instructions:

1. Prepare the Cauliflower:
    - Cut the cauliflower into florets and discard the core. Pulse the cauliflower florets in a food processor until they resemble rice grains. You may need to do this in batches.
2. Stir-Fry:
    - Heat 1 tablespoon of sesame oil in a large skillet or wok over medium-high heat. Add minced garlic and diced onion. Stir-fry for 2-3 minutes until the onion is translucent.
3. Add Vegetables:
    - Add the mixed vegetables to the skillet and stir-fry for another 2-3 minutes until they are tender.
4. Push Vegetables to the Side:
    - Push the cooked vegetables to one side of the skillet, creating an empty space. Pour the beaten eggs into the empty space and scramble them until cooked through.
5. Combine:
    - Mix the scrambled eggs with the vegetables in the skillet.
6. Add Cauliflower Rice:
    - Add the riced cauliflower to the skillet. Drizzle the remaining tablespoon of sesame oil over the cauliflower rice.
7. Season:
    - Pour soy sauce (or tamari) over the cauliflower rice. Add sriracha or chili garlic sauce if desired. Season with salt and pepper to taste.
8. Stir-Fry Until Cooked:
    - Stir-fry everything together for 5-7 minutes until the cauliflower is cooked through but still slightly crunchy.
9. Garnish and Serve:

- Garnish with chopped green onions and serve hot.

Enjoy your flavorful and nutritious cauliflower fried rice!

Salmon and Sweet Potato Cakes

Ingredients:

- 2 medium sweet potatoes, peeled and diced
- 2 cans (14.75 oz each) salmon, drained and flaked (or about 2 cups cooked salmon)
- 1/4 cup green onions, finely chopped
- 2 cloves garlic, minced
- 1/4 cup breadcrumbs (or almond flour for a gluten-free option)
- 1 egg, beaten
- 1 teaspoon smoked paprika
- 1/2 teaspoon dried dill (or 1 tablespoon fresh dill, chopped)
- Salt and pepper, to taste
- 2 tablespoons olive oil, for frying

Instructions:

1. Cook the Sweet Potatoes:
    - Place the diced sweet potatoes in a pot of boiling water. Cook until tender, about 10-15 minutes. Drain well and mash them in a large mixing bowl.
2. Prepare the Mixture:
    - To the mashed sweet potatoes, add the flaked salmon, chopped green onions, minced garlic, breadcrumbs, beaten egg, smoked paprika, dried dill, salt, and pepper. Mix until well combined.
3. Form the Cakes:
    - Divide the mixture into equal portions and shape them into patties, about 1/2-inch thick.
4. Cook the Cakes:
    - Heat olive oil in a large skillet over medium heat.
    - Once the oil is hot, add the salmon and sweet potato cakes to the skillet in batches, being careful not to overcrowd the pan. Cook for 3-4 minutes on each side until golden brown and crispy.
5. Serve:
    - Remove the cooked cakes from the skillet and place them on a plate lined with paper towels to drain any excess oil.
    - Serve the salmon and sweet potato cakes hot, garnished with additional green onions or a dollop of Greek yogurt or sour cream, if desired.

Enjoy these flavorful and nutritious Salmon and Sweet Potato Cakes as a delicious appetizer or main dish!

Turkey and Vegetable Meatloaf

Ingredients:

- 1 lb ground turkey
- 1 cup finely chopped mixed vegetables (such as onions, carrots, bell peppers, and mushrooms)
- 2 cloves garlic, minced
- 1/2 cup breadcrumbs
- 1/4 cup grated Parmesan cheese
- 1/4 cup ketchup
- 1 tablespoon Worcestershire sauce
- 1 teaspoon dried thyme
- 1 teaspoon dried oregano
- 1/2 teaspoon salt
- 1/4 teaspoon black pepper
- 1 egg, beaten

Instructions:

1. Preheat Oven:
    - Preheat your oven to 350°F (175°C). Grease a loaf pan with cooking spray or olive oil.
2. Prepare Vegetables:
    - In a skillet, sauté the mixed vegetables and minced garlic over medium heat until they are softened, about 5-7 minutes. Set aside to cool slightly.
3. Mix Ingredients:
    - In a large mixing bowl, combine the ground turkey, sautéed vegetables, breadcrumbs, grated Parmesan cheese, ketchup, Worcestershire sauce, dried thyme, dried oregano, salt, black pepper, and beaten egg. Mix until well combined.
4. Shape Meatloaf:
    - Transfer the turkey mixture to the prepared loaf pan. Press the mixture into the pan evenly, smoothing the top with a spatula.
5. Bake:
    - Bake the meatloaf in the preheated oven for 45-55 minutes, or until it reaches an internal temperature of 165°F (75°C) and the top is golden brown.
6. Rest and Serve:
    - Remove the meatloaf from the oven and let it rest in the loaf pan for 5-10 minutes before slicing.
    - Slice the meatloaf and serve hot with your favorite sides, such as mashed potatoes and steamed vegetables.

Enjoy your flavorful and nutritious Turkey and Vegetable Meatloaf!

Quinoa and Black Bean Stuffed Peppers

Ingredients:

- 4 large bell peppers, any color
- 1 cup quinoa, rinsed
- 1 can (15 oz) black beans, drained and rinsed
- 1 cup corn kernels (fresh, frozen, or canned)
- 1 small onion, finely chopped
- 2 cloves garlic, minced
- 1 teaspoon ground cumin
- 1 teaspoon chili powder
- 1/2 teaspoon paprika
- Salt and pepper, to taste
- 1 cup shredded cheese (such as cheddar or Monterey Jack)
- Fresh cilantro or parsley, chopped, for garnish (optional)

Instructions:

1. Preheat Oven:
   - Preheat your oven to 375°F (190°C). Grease a baking dish large enough to hold the stuffed peppers.
2. Prepare Peppers:
   - Cut the tops off the bell peppers and remove the seeds and membranes from the inside. Set aside.
3. Cook Quinoa:
   - In a medium saucepan, combine the rinsed quinoa with 2 cups of water. Bring to a boil, then reduce the heat to low, cover, and simmer for 15-20 minutes, or until the quinoa is cooked and the water is absorbed.
4. Prepare Filling:
   - In a large skillet, heat a little olive oil over medium heat. Add the chopped onion and garlic, and cook until softened, about 3-4 minutes.
   - Add the cooked quinoa, black beans, corn, ground cumin, chili powder, paprika, salt, and pepper to the skillet. Stir well to combine and cook for another 3-4 minutes until heated through.
5. Stuff Peppers:
   - Stuff each bell pepper with the quinoa and black bean mixture, pressing down gently to pack the filling.
   - Place the stuffed peppers upright in the prepared baking dish.
6. Bake:
   - Cover the baking dish with foil and bake in the preheated oven for 25-30 minutes, or until the peppers are tender.
7. Add Cheese and Serve:

- Remove the foil from the baking dish. Sprinkle shredded cheese over the tops of the stuffed peppers.
- Return the baking dish to the oven and bake, uncovered, for an additional 5-10 minutes, or until the cheese is melted and bubbly.

8. Garnish and Serve:
   - Remove the stuffed peppers from the oven and let them cool slightly before serving.
   - Garnish with chopped fresh cilantro or parsley, if desired.

Enjoy your flavorful Quinoa and Black Bean Stuffed Peppers!

Chicken and Vegetable Kabobs

Ingredients:

- 1 lb (450g) boneless, skinless chicken breasts, cut into cubes
- 2 bell peppers, cut into chunks (any color you prefer)
- 1 red onion, cut into chunks
- 1 zucchini, sliced into rounds
- 1 cup cherry tomatoes
- 1/4 cup olive oil
- 2 cloves garlic, minced
- 2 tablespoons lemon juice
- 1 teaspoon dried oregano
- 1 teaspoon dried thyme
- Salt and pepper, to taste
- Wooden or metal skewers

Instructions:

1. Marinate the Chicken:
    - In a bowl, whisk together olive oil, minced garlic, lemon juice, dried oregano, dried thyme, salt, and pepper to make the marinade.
    - Add the chicken cubes to the marinade and toss to coat. Cover and refrigerate for at least 30 minutes, or up to 4 hours.
2. Prepare the Vegetables:
    - Cut the bell peppers, red onion, and zucchini into chunks or slices, as desired.
    - If you're using wooden skewers, soak them in water for at least 30 minutes to prevent burning.
3. Assemble the Kabobs:
    - Preheat your grill to medium-high heat.
    - Thread the marinated chicken cubes and prepared vegetables onto the skewers, alternating between the chicken and vegetables.
4. Grill the Kabobs:
    - Lightly oil the grill grates to prevent sticking.
    - Place the assembled kabobs on the preheated grill. Cook for 10-12 minutes, turning occasionally, until the chicken is cooked through and the vegetables are tender and lightly charred.
5. Serve:
    - Once cooked, remove the kabobs from the grill and let them rest for a few minutes.
    - Serve the chicken and vegetable kabobs hot, garnished with fresh herbs if desired.

Enjoy your delicious and colorful chicken and vegetable kabobs!

Moroccan Chickpea Stew

Ingredients:

- 2 tablespoons olive oil
- 1 large onion, finely chopped
- 3 cloves garlic, minced
- 1 tablespoon fresh ginger, grated
- 1 tablespoon ground cumin
- 1 tablespoon ground coriander
- 1 teaspoon ground turmeric
- 1 teaspoon paprika
- 1/2 teaspoon ground cinnamon
- 1/4 teaspoon ground cloves
- 1/4 teaspoon cayenne pepper (adjust to taste)
- 2 carrots, diced
- 2 celery stalks, diced
- 1 bell pepper, diced
- 1 can (14 oz) diced tomatoes
- 1 can (14 oz) chickpeas, drained and rinsed
- 3 cups vegetable broth or water
- 1 cup dried apricots, chopped
- 1/4 cup fresh cilantro or parsley, chopped (for garnish)
- Salt and pepper, to taste
- Cooked couscous or rice, for serving

Instructions:

1. Sauté Aromatics:
    - Heat olive oil in a large pot over medium heat. Add chopped onion and cook until softened, about 5 minutes.
    - Add minced garlic and grated ginger, and cook for another 1-2 minutes until fragrant.
2. Add Spices:
    - Stir in ground cumin, ground coriander, ground turmeric, paprika, ground cinnamon, ground cloves, and cayenne pepper. Cook for 1 minute until the spices are fragrant.
3. Add Vegetables:
    - Add diced carrots, celery, and bell pepper to the pot. Cook for 5 minutes, stirring occasionally, until the vegetables begin to soften.
4. Add Tomatoes and Chickpeas:
    - Pour in the diced tomatoes with their juices and the drained and rinsed chickpeas. Stir to combine.
5. Simmer:

- Pour in the vegetable broth or water. Bring the stew to a simmer, then reduce the heat to low. Cover and let it simmer for about 20-25 minutes, or until the vegetables are tender.
6. Add Apricots:
    - Stir in the chopped dried apricots and let the stew simmer for an additional 5 minutes to allow the flavors to meld together.
7. Season and Serve:
    - Taste the stew and adjust the seasoning with salt and pepper, if needed.
    - Serve the Moroccan Chickpea Stew hot, garnished with chopped fresh cilantro or parsley. Serve with cooked couscous or rice on the side.

Enjoy your comforting and aromatic Moroccan Chickpea Stew!

Grilled Steak with Chimichurri Sauce

Ingredients:

For the Steak:

- 4 steaks of your choice (such as ribeye, sirloin, or flank steak)
- Salt and pepper, to taste
- Olive oil, for brushing

For the Chimichurri Sauce:

- 1 cup fresh parsley, chopped
- 1/4 cup fresh cilantro, chopped
- 4 cloves garlic, minced
- 2 tablespoons red wine vinegar (or white wine vinegar)
- 1/4 cup olive oil
- 1 tablespoon fresh lemon juice
- 1 teaspoon dried oregano
- 1/2 teaspoon red pepper flakes (adjust to taste)
- Salt and pepper, to taste

Instructions:

For the Steak:

1. Preheat Grill:
   - Preheat your grill to high heat.
2. Season Steak:
   - Season both sides of the steaks generously with salt and pepper.
3. Grill Steak:
   - Brush the steaks lightly with olive oil.
   - Place the steaks on the hot grill and cook to your desired level of doneness, flipping once halfway through cooking. Cooking times will vary depending on the thickness of your steaks and your preferred level of doneness. For medium-rare, it usually takes about 4-5 minutes per side.
4. Rest:
   - Once cooked to your liking, transfer the steaks to a plate and let them rest for a few minutes before serving. This allows the juices to redistribute and the steaks to remain juicy.

For the Chimichurri Sauce:

1. Prepare Ingredients:

- In a bowl, combine the chopped parsley, chopped cilantro, minced garlic, red wine vinegar, olive oil, lemon juice, dried oregano, and red pepper flakes. Mix well.
2. Season:
   - Season the chimichurri sauce with salt and pepper to taste. Adjust the seasoning according to your preference.
3. Serve:
   - Serve the grilled steaks hot, topped with a generous spoonful of chimichurri sauce on top or on the side.

Enjoy your delicious Grilled Steak with Chimichurri Sauce! It's a perfect dish for a summer barbecue or any special occasion.

Vegetable and Lentil Shepherd's Pie

Ingredients:

For the Filling:

- 1 cup dried green or brown lentils
- 2 cups vegetable broth or water
- 2 tablespoons olive oil
- 1 onion, chopped
- 2 carrots, diced
- 2 celery stalks, diced
- 2 cloves garlic, minced
- 1 cup mushrooms, chopped
- 1 teaspoon dried thyme
- 1 teaspoon dried rosemary
- 1 teaspoon paprika
- Salt and pepper, to taste
- 1 cup frozen peas
- 1 cup corn kernels (fresh, frozen, or canned)
- 2 tablespoons tomato paste
- 2 tablespoons soy sauce (or tamari for gluten-free)
- 2 tablespoons all-purpose flour (or gluten-free flour)
- 1 cup vegetable broth or water

For the Mashed Potato Topping:

- 4 large potatoes, peeled and diced
- 2 tablespoons butter or olive oil
- 1/4 cup milk or vegetable broth
- Salt and pepper, to taste

Instructions:

For the Filling:

1. Cook Lentils:
   - Rinse the lentils under cold water. In a saucepan, combine the lentils and vegetable broth or water. Bring to a boil, then reduce the heat to low, cover, and simmer for about 20-25 minutes, or until the lentils are tender. Drain any excess liquid and set aside.
2. Sauté Vegetables:
   - In a large skillet, heat olive oil over medium heat. Add chopped onion, diced carrots, and diced celery. Sauté for about 5 minutes, until the vegetables are softened.

- Add minced garlic, chopped mushrooms, dried thyme, dried rosemary, paprika, salt, and pepper. Cook for an additional 2-3 minutes, until the mushrooms are tender.
3. Add Remaining Ingredients:
    - Stir in the cooked lentils, frozen peas, corn kernels, tomato paste, and soy sauce. Cook for another 2-3 minutes, until heated through.
    - In a small bowl, whisk together the all-purpose flour and vegetable broth or water to create a slurry. Pour the slurry into the skillet and stir well. Cook for a few minutes until the filling thickens. Remove from heat and set aside.

For the Mashed Potato Topping:

1. Cook Potatoes:
    - Place the diced potatoes in a large pot of salted water. Bring to a boil, then reduce the heat to medium-low and simmer for about 15-20 minutes, or until the potatoes are fork-tender. Drain well.
2. Mash Potatoes:
    - Return the cooked potatoes to the pot. Add butter or olive oil and milk or vegetable broth. Mash the potatoes using a potato masher until smooth and creamy. Season with salt and pepper to taste.

Assemble and Bake:

1. Preheat Oven:
    - Preheat your oven to 375°F (190°C).
2. Assemble Pie:
    - Transfer the vegetable and lentil filling to a baking dish or pie dish. Spread the mashed potatoes evenly over the top of the filling.
3. Bake:
    - Place the assembled shepherd's pie in the preheated oven and bake for 25-30 minutes, or until the filling is bubbling and the mashed potatoes are golden brown on top.
4. Serve:
    - Remove from the oven and let it cool for a few minutes before serving. Serve hot and enjoy!

This Vegetable and Lentil Shepherd's Pie is a satisfying and nutritious meal that's perfect for a cozy dinner.

Shrimp and Avocado Salad

Ingredients:

For the Salad:

- 1 lb (450g) large shrimp, peeled and deveined
- 2 avocados, diced
- 1 cucumber, diced
- 1 cup cherry tomatoes, halved
- 1/4 cup red onion, thinly sliced
- 1/4 cup fresh cilantro or parsley, chopped
- 1/4 cup crumbled feta cheese (optional)
- Salt and pepper, to taste

For the Dressing:

- 3 tablespoons olive oil
- 2 tablespoons fresh lime juice
- 1 clove garlic, minced
- 1 teaspoon honey or maple syrup
- Salt and pepper, to taste

Instructions:

1. Cook Shrimp:
    - Bring a large pot of salted water to a boil. Add the shrimp and cook for 2-3 minutes, or until they turn pink and opaque. Drain the shrimp and rinse them under cold water to stop the cooking process. Pat them dry with paper towels.
2. Prepare Dressing:
    - In a small bowl, whisk together olive oil, lime juice, minced garlic, honey or maple syrup, salt, and pepper to make the dressing. Set aside.
3. Assemble Salad:
    - In a large mixing bowl, combine the cooked shrimp, diced avocado, diced cucumber, halved cherry tomatoes, thinly sliced red onion, and chopped cilantro or parsley. If using, add crumbled feta cheese to the salad.
4. Add Dressing:
    - Pour the dressing over the salad ingredients. Gently toss to coat everything evenly with the dressing.
5. Season:
    - Taste the salad and adjust the seasoning with salt and pepper, if needed.
6. Serve:
    - Serve the shrimp and avocado salad immediately, garnished with extra cilantro or parsley if desired.

Enjoy your delicious and nutritious Shrimp and Avocado Salad! It's a perfect combination of flavors and textures that's sure to please.

Chicken and Spinach Alfredo

Ingredients:

- 8 oz (225g) fettuccine pasta
- 2 boneless, skinless chicken breasts, thinly sliced
- Salt and pepper, to taste
- 2 tablespoons olive oil
- 2 cloves garlic, minced
- 4 cups fresh spinach leaves
- 1 cup heavy cream
- 1/2 cup grated Parmesan cheese
- 1/4 teaspoon nutmeg (optional)
- Fresh parsley, chopped, for garnish (optional)

Instructions:

1. Cook Pasta:
   - Cook the fettuccine pasta according to the package instructions in a large pot of salted boiling water. Drain the pasta and set aside.
2. Cook Chicken:
   - Season the thinly sliced chicken breasts with salt and pepper to taste.
   - Heat olive oil in a large skillet over medium-high heat. Add the seasoned chicken slices to the skillet and cook for 5-6 minutes on each side, or until golden brown and cooked through. Remove the cooked chicken from the skillet and set aside.
3. Prepare Sauce:
   - In the same skillet, add minced garlic and cook for 1 minute until fragrant. Add fresh spinach leaves to the skillet and cook until wilted, about 2-3 minutes.
4. Add Cream and Cheese:
   - Pour heavy cream into the skillet with the spinach and garlic. Bring the cream to a simmer, then reduce the heat to low.
   - Stir in grated Parmesan cheese and nutmeg (if using). Cook for another 2-3 minutes until the sauce thickens slightly.
5. Combine Pasta and Sauce:
   - Add the cooked fettuccine pasta to the skillet with the creamy spinach sauce. Toss to coat the pasta evenly with the sauce.
6. Add Chicken:
   - Slice the cooked chicken breasts into thin strips. Add the sliced chicken to the skillet with the pasta and sauce. Toss gently to combine.
7. Serve:
   - Serve the chicken and spinach Alfredo hot, garnished with chopped fresh parsley if desired.

Enjoy your creamy and delicious Chicken and Spinach Alfredo pasta! It's perfect for a cozy dinner at home.

Baked Eggplant with Tomato Sauce

Ingredients:

- 2 medium eggplants
- Salt, for sweating
- Olive oil, for brushing
- 2 cups tomato sauce (homemade or store-bought)
- 1 cup shredded mozzarella cheese
- 1/4 cup grated Parmesan cheese
- Fresh basil leaves, chopped, for garnish (optional)

Instructions:

1. Preheat Oven:
    - Preheat your oven to 400°F (200°C). Lightly grease a baking dish with olive oil.
2. Prepare Eggplant:
    - Slice the eggplants into rounds, about 1/4-inch thick. Place the eggplant slices on a paper towel-lined baking sheet and sprinkle both sides generously with salt. Let them sit for about 20-30 minutes to allow the bitter juices to release.
3. Rinse and Pat Dry:
    - After the eggplant slices have sweated, rinse them under cold water to remove the excess salt. Pat them dry with paper towels to remove any moisture.
4. Brush with Olive Oil:
    - Arrange the eggplant slices on the prepared baking dish in a single layer. Brush both sides of the eggplant slices with olive oil.
5. Bake Eggplant:
    - Bake the eggplant slices in the preheated oven for about 15-20 minutes, flipping halfway through, until they are tender and lightly golden brown.
6. Layer with Sauce and Cheese:
    - Remove the baked eggplant slices from the oven. Spoon a layer of tomato sauce over each eggplant slice. Sprinkle shredded mozzarella cheese and grated Parmesan cheese over the tomato sauce.
7. Bake Again:
    - Return the baking dish to the oven and bake for another 10-15 minutes, or until the cheese is melted and bubbly.
8. Serve:
    - Remove the baked eggplant with tomato sauce from the oven and let it cool slightly. Garnish with chopped fresh basil leaves, if desired, before serving.

Enjoy your flavorful Baked Eggplant with Tomato Sauce! It makes a delicious vegetarian main dish or side dish.

Spicy Tofu and Vegetable Stir-Fry

Ingredients:

For the Stir-Fry Sauce:

- 1/4 cup soy sauce (or tamari for gluten-free option)
- 2 tablespoons hoisin sauce
- 1 tablespoon rice vinegar
- 1 tablespoon sesame oil
- 1 tablespoon sriracha sauce (adjust to taste)
- 2 cloves garlic, minced
- 1 teaspoon fresh ginger, grated
- 1 tablespoon cornstarch
- 1/4 cup water

For the Stir-Fry:

- 14 oz (400g) extra-firm tofu, pressed and cubed
- 2 tablespoons vegetable oil
- 2 bell peppers, sliced
- 1 onion, sliced
- 2 cups broccoli florets
- 1 carrot, julienned
- Cooked rice or noodles, for serving
- Sesame seeds and chopped green onions, for garnish (optional)

Instructions:

1. Prepare the Stir-Fry Sauce:
    - In a small bowl, whisk together soy sauce, hoisin sauce, rice vinegar, sesame oil, sriracha sauce, minced garlic, grated ginger, cornstarch, and water until well combined. Set aside.
2. Prepare the Tofu:
    - Press the tofu to remove excess moisture. Cut the pressed tofu into cubes.
3. Stir-Fry Tofu:
    - Heat 1 tablespoon of vegetable oil in a large skillet or wok over medium-high heat. Add the cubed tofu and cook until golden brown on all sides. Remove the tofu from the skillet and set aside.
4. Stir-Fry Vegetables:
    - In the same skillet, heat the remaining tablespoon of vegetable oil. Add sliced bell peppers, sliced onion, broccoli florets, and julienned carrot. Stir-fry for 3-4 minutes until the vegetables are tender-crisp.
5. Combine:
    - Return the cooked tofu to the skillet with the vegetables. Stir well to combine.

6. Add Sauce:
    - Pour the prepared stir-fry sauce over the tofu and vegetables in the skillet. Stir well to coat everything evenly with the sauce.
7. Simmer:
    - Cook for another 2-3 minutes, stirring occasionally, until the sauce has thickened and everything is heated through.
8. Serve:
    - Serve the spicy tofu and vegetable stir-fry hot over cooked rice or noodles.
9. Garnish:
    - Garnish with sesame seeds and chopped green onions, if desired.

Enjoy your delicious and spicy tofu and vegetable stir-fry! Adjust the level of spiciness to your taste by adding more or less sriracha sauce.

Lemon Garlic Shrimp with Zoodles

Ingredients:

For the Lemon Garlic Shrimp:

- 1 lb (450g) large shrimp, peeled and deveined
- 3 cloves garlic, minced
- 2 tablespoons olive oil
- Zest of 1 lemon
- Juice of 1 lemon
- Salt and pepper, to taste
- Fresh parsley, chopped, for garnish (optional)

For the Zoodles:

- 4 medium zucchini
- 2 tablespoons olive oil
- Salt and pepper, to taste

Instructions:

For the Lemon Garlic Shrimp:

1. Marinate Shrimp:
    - In a bowl, combine the peeled and deveined shrimp with minced garlic, olive oil, lemon zest, lemon juice, salt, and pepper. Toss to coat the shrimp evenly with the marinade. Let them marinate for about 15-30 minutes in the refrigerator.
2. Cook Shrimp:
    - Heat a large skillet over medium-high heat. Add the marinated shrimp to the skillet in a single layer, making sure not to overcrowd the pan. Cook for 2-3 minutes on each side, or until the shrimp are pink and opaque.
3. Garnish:
    - Once cooked, remove the shrimp from the skillet and transfer them to a plate. Garnish with chopped fresh parsley, if desired.

For the Zoodles:

1. Prepare Zucchini:
    - Using a spiralizer, spiralize the zucchini into noodles (zoodles). If you don't have a spiralizer, you can use a vegetable peeler to create thin ribbons or simply thinly slice the zucchini lengthwise.
2. Cook Zoodles:

- Heat olive oil in the same skillet used for the shrimp over medium heat. Add the zucchini noodles to the skillet and sauté for 2-3 minutes, tossing occasionally, until they are just tender but still crisp.
3. Season:
   - Season the zoodles with salt and pepper to taste.
4. Serve:
   - Serve the lemon garlic shrimp over the cooked zoodles.

Tips:

- Be careful not to overcook the shrimp, as they can become tough and rubbery.
- You can customize the dish by adding extra vegetables to the zoodles, such as cherry tomatoes or sliced bell peppers, for added flavor and color.
- Feel free to adjust the amount of garlic and lemon according to your taste preferences.

Enjoy your light and flavorful Lemon Garlic Shrimp with Zoodles! It's a perfect dish for a quick and healthy meal.

Turkey and Kale Chili

Ingredients:

- 1 lb (450g) ground turkey
- 1 onion, chopped
- 3 cloves garlic, minced
- 1 bell pepper, diced
- 2 cups chopped kale leaves (stems removed)
- 1 can (14.5 oz) diced tomatoes
- 1 can (15 oz) kidney beans, drained and rinsed
- 1 can (15 oz) black beans, drained and rinsed
- 2 cups chicken or vegetable broth
- 2 tablespoons tomato paste
- 2 teaspoons chili powder
- 1 teaspoon ground cumin
- 1 teaspoon paprika
- 1/2 teaspoon dried oregano
- Salt and pepper, to taste
- Olive oil, for cooking
- Optional toppings: shredded cheese, chopped cilantro, sliced jalapeños, sour cream, avocado slices, lime wedges

Instructions:

1. Cook Ground Turkey:
   - Heat a large pot or Dutch oven over medium heat. Add a little olive oil to the pot.
   - Add the chopped onion and bell pepper to the pot and sauté for 5 minutes until softened.
   - Add the minced garlic and cook for another minute until fragrant.
   - Add the ground turkey to the pot and cook, breaking it apart with a spoon, until it's browned and cooked through.
2. Add Remaining Ingredients:
   - Stir in the chopped kale leaves, diced tomatoes, kidney beans, black beans, chicken or vegetable broth, tomato paste, chili powder, ground cumin, paprika, dried oregano, salt, and pepper.
3. Simmer:
   - Bring the chili to a simmer. Reduce the heat to low, cover, and let it simmer for about 20-25 minutes, stirring occasionally, to allow the flavors to meld together and the kale to soften.
4. Adjust Seasoning:
   - Taste the chili and adjust the seasoning with more salt, pepper, or spices, if needed, according to your taste preferences.
5. Serve:

- Ladle the turkey and kale chili into bowls. Serve hot with your favorite toppings, such as shredded cheese, chopped cilantro, sliced jalapeños, sour cream, avocado slices, or lime wedges.

Enjoy your hearty and nutritious Turkey and Kale Chili! It's a comforting meal that's perfect for chilly evenings.

Grilled Portobello Mushroom Burger

Ingredients:

For the Mushroom Marinade:

- 4 large portobello mushrooms, stems removed
- 1/4 cup balsamic vinegar
- 2 tablespoons olive oil
- 2 cloves garlic, minced
- 1 teaspoon dried thyme
- Salt and pepper, to taste

For the Burger:

- 4 burger buns
- 4 slices Swiss cheese (optional)
- Lettuce leaves
- Sliced tomatoes
- Sliced red onion
- Mayonnaise or your favorite burger sauce
- Mustard (optional)

Instructions:

1. Prepare the Mushroom Marinade:
   - In a shallow dish, whisk together balsamic vinegar, olive oil, minced garlic, dried thyme, salt, and pepper to make the marinade.
2. Marinate the Portobello Mushrooms:
   - Place the portobello mushrooms in the marinade, turning to coat them evenly. Let them marinate for about 20-30 minutes, flipping them halfway through if possible.
3. Preheat the Grill:
   - Preheat your grill to medium-high heat.
4. Grill the Mushrooms:
   - Remove the mushrooms from the marinade and place them on the preheated grill, gill side down. Grill for 5-7 minutes on each side, or until the mushrooms are tender and lightly charred.
5. Toast the Burger Buns:
   - While the mushrooms are grilling, lightly toast the burger buns on the grill for a minute or two, until they are golden brown.
6. Assemble the Burger:
   - Spread mayonnaise or your favorite burger sauce on the bottom half of each toasted bun. Add a lettuce leaf, followed by a grilled portobello mushroom. If desired, add a slice of Swiss cheese on top of each mushroom.

- Top the mushrooms with sliced tomatoes and sliced red onion. Spread mustard on the top half of the burger buns, if using.
- Place the top half of each burger bun on top of the assembled burgers.
7. Serve:
    - Serve the grilled portobello mushroom burgers hot, with your favorite side dishes.

Enjoy your flavorful and satisfying Grilled Portobello Mushroom Burgers! They're a tasty vegetarian alternative for your next barbecue or cookout.

Spinach and Ricotta Stuffed Shells

Ingredients:

For the Stuffed Shells:

- 24 jumbo pasta shells
- 2 cups ricotta cheese
- 1 1/2 cups shredded mozzarella cheese, divided
- 1/2 cup grated Parmesan cheese
- 1 egg
- 1 cup chopped spinach (fresh or frozen, thawed and drained)
- 2 cloves garlic, minced
- 1 teaspoon dried oregano
- 1 teaspoon dried basil
- Salt and pepper, to taste

For the Sauce:

- 3 cups marinara sauce (homemade or store-bought)
- 1/2 cup shredded mozzarella cheese, for topping
- Fresh basil leaves, chopped, for garnish (optional)

Instructions:

1. Cook the Pasta Shells:
    - Cook the jumbo pasta shells according to the package instructions until they are al dente. Drain and set aside to cool slightly.
2. Prepare the Filling:
    - In a large mixing bowl, combine ricotta cheese, 1 cup shredded mozzarella cheese, grated Parmesan cheese, egg, chopped spinach, minced garlic, dried oregano, dried basil, salt, and pepper. Mix until well combined.
3. Stuff the Shells:
    - Preheat your oven to 350°F (175°C). Spread a thin layer of marinara sauce on the bottom of a 9x13-inch baking dish.
    - Spoon the ricotta mixture into the cooked pasta shells, filling each shell generously.
4. Assemble the Dish:
    - Arrange the stuffed shells in the prepared baking dish, nestled closely together.
    - Pour the remaining marinara sauce over the stuffed shells, covering them evenly. Sprinkle the remaining 1/2 cup shredded mozzarella cheese on top.
5. Bake:
    - Cover the baking dish with aluminum foil and bake in the preheated oven for 25-30 minutes, or until the sauce is bubbly and the cheese is melted.
6. Serve:

- Remove the foil from the baking dish and bake for an additional 5-10 minutes, until the cheese is golden brown and bubbly.
- Garnish with chopped fresh basil leaves, if desired, before serving.

Enjoy your delicious Spinach and Ricotta Stuffed Shells! They make a satisfying and comforting meal for any occasion.

Chicken and Sweet Potato Curry

Ingredients:

- 1 lb (450g) boneless, skinless chicken breasts or thighs, cut into bite-sized pieces
- 2 tablespoons olive oil or vegetable oil
- 1 onion, finely chopped
- 3 cloves garlic, minced
- 1 tablespoon fresh ginger, grated
- 2 tablespoons curry powder
- 1 teaspoon ground cumin
- 1 teaspoon ground coriander
- 1/2 teaspoon turmeric
- 1/4 teaspoon cayenne pepper (optional, for extra heat)
- 2 large sweet potatoes, peeled and diced into cubes
- 1 can (14 oz) diced tomatoes
- 1 can (14 oz) coconut milk
- 1 cup chicken broth
- Salt and pepper, to taste
- Fresh cilantro, chopped, for garnish (optional)
- Cooked rice or naan bread, for serving

Instructions:

1. Sauté Chicken:
    - Heat olive oil or vegetable oil in a large pot or Dutch oven over medium-high heat. Add the chopped onion and cook until softened, about 5 minutes.
    - Add the minced garlic and grated ginger to the pot and cook for another minute until fragrant.
    - Add the chicken pieces to the pot and cook until browned on all sides, about 5-7 minutes.
2. Add Spices:
    - Sprinkle curry powder, ground cumin, ground coriander, turmeric, and cayenne pepper (if using) over the chicken. Stir well to coat the chicken with the spices.
3. Cook Sweet Potatoes:
    - Add the diced sweet potatoes to the pot and stir to combine with the chicken and spices.
4. Simmer:
    - Pour in the diced tomatoes (with their juices), coconut milk, and chicken broth. Stir well to combine. Season with salt and pepper, to taste.
    - Bring the curry to a simmer, then reduce the heat to low. Cover and let it simmer for about 20-25 minutes, or until the sweet potatoes are tender and the chicken is cooked through.
5. Adjust Seasoning:

        - Taste the curry and adjust the seasoning with more salt and pepper, if needed.
6. Serve:
    - Serve the chicken and sweet potato curry hot, garnished with chopped fresh cilantro, if desired. Serve with cooked rice or naan bread on the side.

Enjoy your flavorful and comforting Chicken and Sweet Potato Curry! It's a perfect dish for a cozy dinner at home.

Zucchini and Corn Fritters

Ingredients:

- 2 medium zucchinis, grated
- 1 cup corn kernels (fresh, frozen, or canned)
- 1/2 cup all-purpose flour
- 1/4 cup grated Parmesan cheese
- 2 green onions, finely chopped
- 2 cloves garlic, minced
- 2 eggs, lightly beaten
- 1/2 teaspoon baking powder
- Salt and pepper, to taste
- Olive oil, for frying

Instructions:

1. Prepare Zucchini:
   - Grate the zucchinis using a box grater. Place the grated zucchini in a clean kitchen towel or cheesecloth and squeeze out excess moisture.
2. Mix Ingredients:
   - In a large mixing bowl, combine the grated zucchini, corn kernels, all-purpose flour, grated Parmesan cheese, chopped green onions, minced garlic, beaten eggs, baking powder, salt, and pepper. Stir until well combined.
3. Heat Oil:
   - Heat a thin layer of olive oil in a large skillet or frying pan over medium heat.
4. Cook Fritters:
   - Drop spoonfuls of the zucchini and corn mixture into the hot oil, using a tablespoon or an ice cream scoop to form fritters. Flatten them slightly with the back of the spoon.
   - Cook the fritters in batches for 2-3 minutes on each side, or until golden brown and crispy. Adjust the heat if necessary to prevent them from burning.
5. Drain:
   - Once cooked, transfer the fritters to a plate lined with paper towels to drain off any excess oil.
6. Serve:
   - Serve the zucchini and corn fritters hot, garnished with additional chopped green onions or grated Parmesan cheese if desired. You can also serve them with a dipping sauce such as sour cream, yogurt, or salsa.

Enjoy your delicious and crispy Zucchini and Corn Fritters! They're perfect for any occasion and are sure to be a hit with family and friends.

Baked Tilapia with Steamed Vegetables

Ingredients:

For the Baked Tilapia:

- 4 tilapia fillets
- 2 tablespoons olive oil
- 2 cloves garlic, minced
- 1 teaspoon paprika
- 1 teaspoon dried thyme
- Salt and pepper, to taste
- Lemon wedges, for serving

For the Steamed Vegetables:

- Assorted vegetables of your choice (such as broccoli, carrots, green beans, bell peppers, or zucchini), washed and chopped
- Salt, to taste
- Lemon juice, for drizzling (optional)
- Fresh herbs (such as parsley or dill), chopped, for garnish (optional)

Instructions:

For the Baked Tilapia:

1. Preheat Oven:
    - Preheat your oven to 400°F (200°C).
2. Prepare Tilapia:
    - Pat the tilapia fillets dry with paper towels. Place them on a baking sheet lined with parchment paper or aluminum foil.
3. Season Tilapia:
    - In a small bowl, combine olive oil, minced garlic, paprika, dried thyme, salt, and pepper. Stir well to make a marinade.
    - Brush the marinade over the tilapia fillets, coating them evenly.
4. Bake Tilapia:
    - Bake the tilapia fillets in the preheated oven for 12-15 minutes, or until the fish is cooked through and flakes easily with a fork.
5. Serve:
    - Remove the baked tilapia from the oven and serve hot, garnished with lemon wedges.

For the Steamed Vegetables:

1. Prepare Steamer:

- Meanwhile, prepare a steamer basket or pot with a steamer insert. Fill the bottom of the pot with water, making sure it doesn't touch the steamer basket.
2. Steam Vegetables:
    - Place the chopped vegetables in the steamer basket. Season with salt, if desired.
    - Cover the pot with a lid and steam the vegetables for 5-7 minutes, or until they are tender but still crisp.
3. Serve:
    - Transfer the steamed vegetables to a serving dish. Drizzle with lemon juice, if desired, and garnish with chopped fresh herbs.

Enjoy your healthy and flavorful Baked Tilapia with Steamed Vegetables! It's a nutritious meal that's perfect for any day of the week.

Quinoa and Avocado Salad

Ingredients:

For the Salad:

- 1 cup quinoa, rinsed
- 2 cups water or vegetable broth
- 1 ripe avocado, diced
- 1 cup cherry tomatoes, halved
- 1/2 cucumber, diced
- 1/4 cup red onion, finely chopped
- 1/4 cup fresh cilantro or parsley, chopped
- 1/4 cup crumbled feta cheese (optional)
- Salt and pepper, to taste

For the Dressing:

- 3 tablespoons extra virgin olive oil
- 2 tablespoons fresh lemon juice
- 1 clove garlic, minced
- 1 teaspoon Dijon mustard
- Salt and pepper, to taste

Instructions:

1. Cook Quinoa:
   - In a medium saucepan, combine quinoa and water or vegetable broth. Bring to a boil, then reduce the heat to low, cover, and simmer for about 15 minutes, or until the quinoa is cooked and the liquid is absorbed. Remove from heat and let it cool slightly.
2. Prepare Dressing:
   - In a small bowl, whisk together extra virgin olive oil, fresh lemon juice, minced garlic, Dijon mustard, salt, and pepper to make the dressing. Set aside.
3. Assemble Salad:
   - In a large mixing bowl, combine the cooked quinoa, diced avocado, halved cherry tomatoes, diced cucumber, finely chopped red onion, and chopped fresh cilantro or parsley. If using, add crumbled feta cheese to the salad.
4. Add Dressing:
   - Pour the dressing over the salad ingredients. Toss gently to coat everything evenly with the dressing.
5. Season:
   - Taste the salad and adjust the seasoning with salt and pepper, if needed.
6. Serve:

- Serve the quinoa and avocado salad immediately, or refrigerate for about 30 minutes to allow the flavors to meld together before serving.

Enjoy your nutritious and flavorful Quinoa and Avocado Salad! It's packed with protein, fiber, and healthy fats, making it a satisfying and wholesome meal option.

Grilled Lamb Chops with Mint Yogurt

Ingredients:

For the Lamb Chops:

- 8 lamb chops, about 1 inch thick
- 2 tablespoons olive oil
- 4 cloves garlic, minced
- 2 teaspoons dried oregano
- 2 teaspoons dried thyme
- Salt and pepper, to taste

For the Mint Yogurt Sauce:

- 1 cup Greek yogurt
- 1/4 cup fresh mint leaves, finely chopped
- 1 tablespoon lemon juice
- 1 clove garlic, minced
- Salt and pepper, to taste

For Garnish (optional):

- Fresh mint leaves
- Lemon wedges

Instructions:

For the Lamb Chops:

1. Marinate Lamb Chops:
    - In a shallow dish, combine olive oil, minced garlic, dried oregano, dried thyme, salt, and pepper. Mix well to create a marinade.
    - Add the lamb chops to the marinade, turning to coat them evenly. Cover and refrigerate for at least 30 minutes, or up to 4 hours, to allow the flavors to meld.
2. Preheat Grill:
    - Preheat your grill to medium-high heat.
3. Grill Lamb Chops:
    - Remove the lamb chops from the marinade and discard any excess marinade.
    - Grill the lamb chops for 3-4 minutes per side, or until they reach your desired level of doneness. For medium-rare, the internal temperature should be around 145°F (63°C).
4. Rest:
    - Remove the grilled lamb chops from the grill and let them rest for a few minutes before serving.

For the Mint Yogurt Sauce:

1. Prepare Mint Yogurt Sauce:
   - In a small bowl, combine Greek yogurt, finely chopped fresh mint leaves, lemon juice, minced garlic, salt, and pepper. Stir well to combine.
2. Adjust Seasoning:
   - Taste the mint yogurt sauce and adjust the seasoning with salt and pepper, if needed.

Serving:

1. Serve:
   - Serve the grilled lamb chops hot, accompanied by the mint yogurt sauce on the side.
   - Garnish with fresh mint leaves and lemon wedges, if desired.

Enjoy your delicious Grilled Lamb Chops with Mint Yogurt Sauce! It's a flavorful and elegant dish that's sure to impress your guests.

Roasted Brussels Sprouts and Bacon

Ingredients:

- 1 lb (450g) Brussels sprouts, trimmed and halved
- 4 slices bacon, chopped
- 2 tablespoons olive oil
- Salt and pepper, to taste
- 2 cloves garlic, minced (optional)
- 1 tablespoon balsamic vinegar (optional)
- Grated Parmesan cheese, for serving (optional)
- Chopped fresh parsley, for garnish (optional)

Instructions:

1. Preheat Oven:
    - Preheat your oven to 400°F (200°C).
2. Prepare Brussels Sprouts:
    - Trim the ends of the Brussels sprouts and cut them in half lengthwise.
3. Cook Bacon:
    - In a large oven-safe skillet or baking dish, cook the chopped bacon over medium heat until it starts to render its fat and becomes crispy, about 5-7 minutes.
4. Roast Brussels Sprouts:
    - Add the halved Brussels sprouts to the skillet with the bacon, tossing to coat them in the rendered bacon fat. If needed, add a drizzle of olive oil to ensure the Brussels sprouts are evenly coated.
    - Season with salt and pepper, to taste. Optionally, add minced garlic for extra flavor.
    - Transfer the skillet to the preheated oven and roast for 20-25 minutes, stirring halfway through, or until the Brussels sprouts are tender and caramelized around the edges.
5. Finish and Serve:
    - Once roasted, remove the skillet from the oven. Optionally, drizzle with balsamic vinegar for a tangy flavor.
    - Serve the roasted Brussels sprouts and bacon hot, garnished with grated Parmesan cheese and chopped fresh parsley if desired.

Enjoy your delicious Roasted Brussels Sprouts and Bacon as a side dish or a flavorful addition to any meal!

Beef and Vegetable Skillet

Ingredients:

- 1 lb (450g) lean ground beef
- 2 tablespoons olive oil
- 1 onion, diced
- 2 cloves garlic, minced
- 2 bell peppers (any color), diced
- 2 carrots, peeled and diced
- 2 cups broccoli florets
- 1 cup sliced mushrooms
- 1 teaspoon dried thyme
- 1 teaspoon dried oregano
- Salt and pepper, to taste
- 2 tablespoons soy sauce or Worcestershire sauce
- 1/4 cup beef broth or water
- Cooked rice or quinoa, for serving (optional)
- Chopped fresh parsley, for garnish (optional)

Instructions:

1. Cook Ground Beef:
    - Heat olive oil in a large skillet or frying pan over medium heat. Add the ground beef and cook, breaking it apart with a spoon, until it's browned and cooked through. Drain any excess fat, if needed.
2. Add Aromatics:
    - Add the diced onion and minced garlic to the skillet with the cooked ground beef. Cook for 2-3 minutes, until the onion is softened and the garlic is fragrant.
3. Cook Vegetables:
    - Add the diced bell peppers, diced carrots, broccoli florets, and sliced mushrooms to the skillet. Stir well to combine.
    - Season the vegetables and beef with dried thyme, dried oregano, salt, and pepper, to taste. Cook for 5-7 minutes, stirring occasionally, until the vegetables are tender-crisp.
4. Finish:
    - Stir in soy sauce or Worcestershire sauce and beef broth or water. Cook for another 2-3 minutes, allowing the flavors to meld together.
5. Serve:
    - Serve the beef and vegetable skillet hot, either on its own or over cooked rice or quinoa, if desired.
    - Garnish with chopped fresh parsley for a pop of color and freshness.

Enjoy your delicious and nutritious Beef and Vegetable Skillet! It's a satisfying meal that's perfect for busy weeknights.

Chicken Caesar Salad Wrap

Ingredients:

- 2 boneless, skinless chicken breasts
- Salt and pepper, to taste
- 2 tablespoons olive oil
- 4 large flour tortillas or wraps
- 2 cups romaine lettuce, chopped
- 1/4 cup grated Parmesan cheese
- 1/2 cup Caesar salad dressing (homemade or store-bought)
- 1/2 cup croutons
- Lemon wedges, for serving (optional)

Instructions:

1. Cook Chicken:
    - Season the chicken breasts with salt and pepper, to taste. In a large skillet over medium-high heat, heat olive oil. Add the seasoned chicken breasts and cook for 6-7 minutes per side, or until cooked through and no longer pink in the center. Remove from heat and let them cool slightly.
2. Slice Chicken:
    - Once cooled, slice the cooked chicken breasts into thin strips or cubes.
3. Assemble Wraps:
    - Lay out the flour tortillas or wraps on a clean work surface.
    - Divide the chopped romaine lettuce evenly among the tortillas, spreading it out in a line down the center of each wrap.
    - Sprinkle grated Parmesan cheese over the lettuce on each wrap.
    - Arrange the sliced cooked chicken over the lettuce and cheese on each wrap.
4. Add Dressing and Croutons:
    - Drizzle Caesar salad dressing over the chicken on each wrap.
    - Sprinkle croutons over the dressing on each wrap.
5. Wrap:
    - To wrap each chicken Caesar salad wrap, fold the sides of the tortilla over the filling, then roll it up tightly from the bottom.
6. Serve:
    - Serve the chicken Caesar salad wraps immediately, or wrap them tightly in foil or parchment paper for later. If desired, serve with lemon wedges on the side for squeezing over the wraps before eating.

Enjoy your delicious and convenient Chicken Caesar Salad Wraps! They're perfect for a quick lunch or on-the-go meal.

Tofu and Vegetable Kebabs

Ingredients:

- 1 block (14 oz) firm tofu, pressed and cut into cubes
- 2 bell peppers (any color), cut into chunks
- 1 red onion, cut into chunks
- 1 zucchini, sliced into rounds
- 1 cup cherry tomatoes
- 8-10 wooden skewers, soaked in water for at least 30 minutes

For the Marinade:

- 1/4 cup soy sauce
- 2 tablespoons olive oil
- 2 tablespoons maple syrup or honey
- 2 cloves garlic, minced
- 1 teaspoon ground ginger
- 1/2 teaspoon ground black pepper
- 1 tablespoon chopped fresh herbs (such as parsley, thyme, or rosemary) - optional

Instructions:

1. Prepare Marinade:
    - In a small bowl, whisk together soy sauce, olive oil, maple syrup or honey, minced garlic, ground ginger, black pepper, and chopped fresh herbs (if using). Set aside.
2. Marinate Tofu:
    - Place the cubed tofu in a shallow dish or resealable plastic bag. Pour the marinade over the tofu, making sure it's well coated. Marinate in the refrigerator for at least 30 minutes, or up to 2 hours, to allow the flavors to develop.
3. Prepare Vegetables:
    - While the tofu is marinating, prepare the vegetables. Cut the bell peppers, red onion, zucchini, and cherry tomatoes into chunks or slices as desired.
4. Assemble Kebabs:
    - Thread the marinated tofu cubes and prepared vegetables onto the soaked wooden skewers, alternating the ingredients as desired.
5. Cook Kebabs:
    - If grilling: Preheat the grill to medium-high heat. Grill the tofu and vegetable kebabs for 10-12 minutes, turning occasionally, until the tofu is lightly browned and the vegetables are tender.
    - If baking: Preheat the oven to 400°F (200°C). Place the assembled kebabs on a baking sheet lined with parchment paper. Bake for 20-25 minutes, turning once halfway through cooking, until the tofu is lightly browned and the vegetables are tender.

6. Serve:
    - Once cooked, remove the tofu and vegetable kebabs from the grill or oven. Serve hot, garnished with additional chopped fresh herbs if desired.

Enjoy your flavorful and colorful Tofu and Vegetable Kebabs! They're perfect for a vegetarian barbecue or a weeknight dinner.

Barley and Mushroom Soup

Ingredients:

- 1 cup pearl barley
- 8 cups vegetable or chicken broth
- 2 tablespoons olive oil
- 1 onion, diced
- 3 cloves garlic, minced
- 2 carrots, diced
- 2 celery stalks, diced
- 8 oz (225g) mushrooms, sliced
- 1 teaspoon dried thyme
- 1 teaspoon dried rosemary
- Salt and pepper, to taste
- Chopped fresh parsley, for garnish (optional)

Instructions:

1. Rinse Barley:
    - Rinse the pearl barley under cold water in a fine-mesh sieve and drain well.
2. Cook Barley:
    - In a large pot or Dutch oven, bring the vegetable or chicken broth to a boil. Add the rinsed barley to the boiling broth.
    - Reduce the heat to low, cover, and simmer for about 30-40 minutes, or until the barley is tender. Drain any excess liquid and set the cooked barley aside.
3. Sauté Vegetables:
    - In the same pot or Dutch oven, heat olive oil over medium heat. Add the diced onion and minced garlic, and sauté for 2-3 minutes until fragrant.
    - Add the diced carrots and celery to the pot, and cook for another 5 minutes until they begin to soften.
4. Add Mushrooms and Herbs:
    - Add the sliced mushrooms to the pot and cook for 5-7 minutes, or until they are tender and browned.
    - Stir in dried thyme, dried rosemary, salt, and pepper to taste, and cook for another minute to allow the flavors to meld together.
5. Combine Barley and Vegetables:
    - Add the cooked barley to the pot with the sautéed vegetables and mushrooms. Stir well to combine.
6. Simmer Soup:
    - Pour the vegetable or chicken broth over the barley and vegetable mixture in the pot. Bring the soup to a simmer over medium-low heat. Let it simmer for another 10-15 minutes to allow the flavors to develop.
7. Adjust Seasoning and Serve:

- - Taste the soup and adjust the seasoning with more salt and pepper, if needed.
  - Ladle the barley and mushroom soup into bowls. Garnish with chopped fresh parsley, if desired, before serving.

Enjoy your delicious and nourishing Barley and Mushroom Soup! It's a comforting meal that's perfect for lunch or dinner.

Stuffed Acorn Squash

Ingredients:

- 2 acorn squash
- 1 tablespoon olive oil
- Salt and pepper, to taste
- 1 cup quinoa, cooked (or rice, couscous, or any grain of your choice)
- 1 tablespoon butter or olive oil
- 1 small onion, diced
- 2 cloves garlic, minced
- 1 bell pepper, diced
- 1 cup diced mushrooms
- 1/2 cup dried cranberries or raisins
- 1/4 cup chopped fresh parsley or cilantro
- 1/4 cup chopped nuts (such as pecans, walnuts, or almonds)
- 1/4 teaspoon ground cinnamon (optional)
- 1/4 teaspoon ground nutmeg (optional)
- 1/4 cup grated Parmesan cheese (optional)
- Additional toppings: crumbled feta cheese, chopped fresh herbs, balsamic glaze, etc. (optional)

Instructions:

1. Preheat Oven:
   - Preheat your oven to 400°F (200°C).
2. Prepare Acorn Squash:
   - Cut each acorn squash in half lengthwise and scoop out the seeds and stringy pulp.
   - Brush the cut sides of the squash halves with olive oil and season with salt and pepper.
3. Roast Squash:
   - Place the squash halves, cut side down, on a baking sheet lined with parchment paper. Roast in the preheated oven for about 30-40 minutes, or until the squash is tender when pierced with a fork.
4. Prepare Filling:
   - While the squash is roasting, prepare the filling. Heat butter or olive oil in a skillet over medium heat. Add diced onion and minced garlic, and cook until softened and fragrant, about 3-4 minutes.
   - Add diced bell pepper and mushrooms to the skillet, and cook for another 5-7 minutes, or until the vegetables are tender.
5. Combine Ingredients:
   - In a large mixing bowl, combine cooked quinoa (or your choice of grain), cooked vegetable mixture, dried cranberries or raisins, chopped fresh parsley or cilantro,

chopped nuts, ground cinnamon, ground nutmeg, and grated Parmesan cheese (if using). Mix well to combine.
6. Stuff Squash:
    - Once the squash halves are roasted and tender, remove them from the oven and flip them over.
    - Divide the quinoa and vegetable mixture evenly among the squash halves, pressing down gently to pack the filling.
7. Bake Again:
    - Return the stuffed squash to the oven and bake for an additional 10-15 minutes, or until the filling is heated through and the tops are slightly golden.
8. Serve:
    - Once cooked, remove the stuffed acorn squash from the oven. Serve hot, optionally topped with additional toppings such as crumbled feta cheese, chopped fresh herbs, or a drizzle of balsamic glaze.

Enjoy your delicious and nutritious Stuffed Acorn Squash! It's a perfect vegetarian meal for any occasion.

Grilled Chicken with Mango Salsa

Ingredients:

For the Grilled Chicken:

- 4 boneless, skinless chicken breasts
- 2 tablespoons olive oil
- 2 cloves garlic, minced
- 1 teaspoon paprika
- 1 teaspoon ground cumin
- 1 teaspoon dried oregano
- Salt and pepper, to taste

For the Mango Salsa:

- 2 ripe mangos, peeled, pitted, and diced
- 1/2 red onion, finely chopped
- 1 red bell pepper, diced
- 1 jalapeño pepper, seeded and minced
- 1/4 cup fresh cilantro, chopped
- Juice of 1 lime
- Salt and pepper, to taste

For Garnish:

- Fresh cilantro leaves
- Lime wedges

Instructions:

For the Grilled Chicken:

1. Marinate Chicken:
    - In a bowl, combine olive oil, minced garlic, paprika, ground cumin, dried oregano, salt, and pepper. Mix well to make a marinade.
    - Add the chicken breasts to the marinade, turning to coat them evenly. Cover and refrigerate for at least 30 minutes, or up to 4 hours.
2. Preheat Grill:
    - Preheat your grill to medium-high heat.
3. Grill Chicken:
    - Remove the chicken breasts from the marinade and discard any excess marinade.

- Grill the chicken breasts for 6-8 minutes per side, or until they are cooked through and no longer pink in the center. The internal temperature should reach 165°F (75°C).
- Remove the chicken from the grill and let it rest for a few minutes before serving.

For the Mango Salsa:

1. Prepare Mango Salsa:
   - In a bowl, combine diced mango, finely chopped red onion, diced red bell pepper, minced jalapeño pepper, chopped fresh cilantro, lime juice, salt, and pepper. Mix well to combine.
2. Adjust Seasoning:
   - Taste the mango salsa and adjust the seasoning with more salt, pepper, or lime juice, if needed.

Serving:

1. Serve:
   - Serve the grilled chicken breasts hot, topped with mango salsa.
   - Garnish with fresh cilantro leaves and lime wedges on the side.

Enjoy your delicious Grilled Chicken with Mango Salsa! It's a perfect combination of flavors and textures that's sure to impress.

Baked Spaghetti with Spinach and Ricotta

Ingredients:

- 12 oz (340g) spaghetti
- 2 tablespoons olive oil
- 4 cloves garlic, minced
- 1 onion, chopped
- 1 (28 oz) can crushed tomatoes
- 1 teaspoon dried oregano
- 1 teaspoon dried basil
- Salt and pepper, to taste
- 2 cups fresh spinach leaves, chopped
- 1 cup ricotta cheese
- 1 cup shredded mozzarella cheese
- 1/4 cup grated Parmesan cheese
- Fresh basil leaves, for garnish (optional)

Instructions:

1. Preheat Oven:
    - Preheat your oven to 375°F (190°C). Grease a 9x13-inch baking dish with cooking spray or olive oil.
2. Cook Spaghetti:
    - Cook the spaghetti according to the package instructions until al dente. Drain and set aside.
3. Prepare Sauce:
    - In a large skillet, heat olive oil over medium heat. Add minced garlic and chopped onion, and cook until softened and fragrant, about 3-4 minutes.
    - Add the crushed tomatoes, dried oregano, dried basil, salt, and pepper to the skillet. Stir well to combine. Let the sauce simmer for 10-15 minutes, stirring occasionally, to allow the flavors to meld together.
4. Add Spinach:
    - Add the chopped fresh spinach leaves to the skillet with the tomato sauce. Cook for another 2-3 minutes, or until the spinach wilts down and is incorporated into the sauce.
5. Combine Pasta and Sauce:
    - Add the cooked spaghetti to the skillet with the spinach and tomato sauce. Toss well to coat the spaghetti evenly with the sauce.
6. Layer in Baking Dish:
    - Transfer half of the spaghetti mixture to the prepared baking dish, spreading it out evenly. Dollop half of the ricotta cheese over the spaghetti in small spoonfuls. Sprinkle half of the shredded mozzarella cheese and grated Parmesan cheese over the ricotta cheese.

- Repeat the layers with the remaining spaghetti mixture, ricotta cheese, shredded mozzarella cheese, and grated Parmesan cheese.
7. Bake:
    - Cover the baking dish with aluminum foil and bake in the preheated oven for 20 minutes.
    - Remove the foil and bake for an additional 10 minutes, or until the cheese is melted and bubbly, and the edges are golden brown.
8. Serve:
    - Remove the baked spaghetti from the oven and let it cool for a few minutes before serving.
    - Garnish with fresh basil leaves, if desired, and serve hot.

Enjoy your delicious Baked Spaghetti with Spinach and Ricotta! It's a comforting and satisfying meal that's sure to be a hit with the whole family.

www.ingramcontent.com/pod-product-compliance
Lightning Source LLC
LaVergne TN
LVHW081609060526
838201LV00054B/2167